IT'S JUST AN EVENT— IT'S YOUR CHOICE HOW YOU WANT TO FEEL

THE ABC SYSTEM OF COGNITIVE, EMOTIONAL AND BEHAVIORAL SELF-MANAGEMENT AND SELF-IMPROVEMENT

RAY MATHIS

PublishAmerica
Baltimore

First printing

PublishAmerica has allowed this work to remain exactly as the author intended, verbatim, without editorial input.

This publication contains the opinions and ideas of its author. Author intends to offer information of a general nature. Any reliance on the information herein is at the reader's own discretion.

The author and publisher specifically disclaim all responsibility for any liability, loss, or right, personal or otherwise, which is incurred as a consequence, directly or indirectly, of the use and application of any contents of this book. They further make no representations or warranties with respect to the accuracy or completeness of the contents of this work and specifically disclaim all warranties including without limitation any implied warranty of fitness for a particular purpose. Any recommendations are made without any guarantee on the part of the author or the publisher.

ISBN: 978-1-61546-156-1
PUBLISHED BY PUBLISHAMERICA, LLLP
www.publishamerica.com
Baltimore

Printed in the United States of America

I dedicate this book to my wife Jay, who tolerated years of my being on the computer trying to perfect the lessons for my students that led to this book, and to my daughter Erin, who is and always will be my hero.

ACKNOWLEDGMENTS

I sincerely hope you will benefit from this book. If you do, it's because I stood on the shoulders of giants to write it.

My first introduction to what is in this book was from a good friend named Jerry Rankin. Jerry was a counselor at my school and was the first person to ever mention Dr. Albert Ellis and his ABC Theory of Emotions. However, it was not until I met and took classes with Terry London midway through my career that I actually learned the ABC Theory and what is called Rational Emotive Behavioral Therapy (REBT) and Education (REBE), and what I could do to not only help my students, but myself as well.

Terry is a practicing psychotherapist in the Chicago area. He is the co-director of the Rational Emotive Behavioral Institute of Chicago and also teaches over thirty classes through Pearson Education, most of them based on REBT and REBE. He is the most well read, best informed, most knowledgeable, logical and rational instructor I have ever had.

I am sure Terry would be the first to say that he also stood on the shoulders of a giant. That giant would be Dr. Albert Ellis, one of the most prominent psychotherapists of the 20th century, and founder of the Albert Ellis Institute for Rational Emotive Behavioral Therapy in New York City. I had a poster in my room that said, "Genius is looking at what everyone else has looked at, and seeing what no one else has seen". So it was with Dr. Ellis. His ABC Theory of Emotions was truly the product of genius, of someone looking at what so many others had looked at, and seeing what no one else had seen. I am sure Terry believes he owes Dr. Ellis much, and I in turn do too. He is the original giant whose shoulders Terry stood on, and Terry is the giant whose shoulders I stood on.

Unfortunately, before I was able to share a copy of this book with Dr. Ellis, he passed away at the age of 93. He spent his entire life teaching people how to think more rationally, generate a more functional amount of emotion, and act in their own self-interest to make the best of their lives. The least Terry, I, and others can do is pass on what he taught us and carry on his work.

TABLE OF CONTENTS

Introduction

How healthy, happy, hopeful, successful and productive people are, or will be in the future, will depend more than anything else on how they manage what goes on inside their own heads in response to the life events they are confronted with. It depends more than anything else on the thoughts and feelings they generate in response to those events. What people end up saying and doing because of those thoughts and feelings, is often not what they know to be best for themselves, and often has little to do with any good advice or information they have received. It is sometimes even contrary to their personal morals and values. People not being able to effectively manage the thoughts and feelings they generate in response to their life events plays an important role in so much that goes wrong in the lives of individuals, in families and schools, and in our society as a whole.

There are five life skills that are important for all people to learn. These are skills we could and should be teaching people of all ages, especially our young people. Unfortunately, these skills are not being taught in families or schools, or anywhere else for that matter. These skills are:

1) To have an Internal Locus of Control
2) To recognize and correct irrational thinking in oneself and others
3) To have Unconditional Self-Acceptance (U.S.A.) and Unconditional Other-Acceptance (U.O.A.)
4) To have truly effective Emotional Management
5) A step-by-step process by which to approach any potentially troublesome life situation that would allow a person to get into the best possible cognitive (thinking) and emotional place to make the best possible choice for him or herself and others

Teaching people these five life skills is the goal of this book. Each one of these skills, and how to develop them, will be explained in detail in the chapters of this book.

THE PROBLEM

I was a health education teacher for thirty-three years. The medical sciences know more than ever before about how diseases and other problems occur, and how to prevent them. They know more than ever before about how to live longer, healthier, happier and more productive lives. People receive more helpful information and advice than ever before in ever more clever, entertaining and effective ways. Yet there are still way too many people starting and continuing to behave in unhealthy, self-defeating ways, and suffering needlessly, and even dying prematurely because of it, or sometimes causing others to. Most people know someone who does or has, and that person is often a family member or close friend. Despite all the books, magazines, radio and TV programs giving helpful advice and information on how to live longer, be healthy, feel better and have good relationships, millions of people still struggle to do so.

Teachers also know more than ever before about how students learn, and how to best teach them, and to accommodate those with special needs. Despite what some think, teachers teach and accommodate those with special needs better than ever before. Yet there are still way too many students who function at levels below what they are capable of, and than their teachers, parents and perhaps even they would like. There are also too many others dropping out.

Hundreds of self-help books, magazines and newspapers articles, TV and radio programs, textbooks and curriculums, community and school-based programs have tried to target one or more of the problems individuals, families, schools and society face. They have all given people plenty of helpful information and advice. They have even sometimes taught people helpful skills such as problem solving, conflict resolution, assertiveness, and how to communicate more effectively. Others have even promoted helpful values and morals. However, people have to be in the right cognitive and emotional place to access and act on helpful information and advice, and to perform helpful skills they have learned. People also have to be in the right cognitive and emotional place to learn from their own and others experiences, to consider consequences before acting, and to act in a way that is consistent with the morals and values they have received from their family and religion. These many books, magazines and programs have largely neglected to show people how to get there.

Teaching people how to get into the best possible cognitive and emotional place is a major goal of this book. The goal is to help people free themselves to make the healthiest possible choices for themselves and others. It is to free people to act in their own best self-interest and the interest of others as often as possible. I like to call the ability to do so mental and emotional fitness.

It has been said that there are two ways to make an already bad situation worse, do nothing and overreact to it. More often than not, people react rather than respond, and often overreact. Responsibility (response-ability) actually means the ability to respond to life events rather than react to them. The goal of this book is to help people become truly response-able, or able to respond to their life events rather than react to them. At the same time, it is to make people less disturb-able, or less able to be as easily and unnecessarily disturbed by their life events as they are now.

QUESTIONS AND ANSWERS

Why do people start and continue to behave in unhealthy, self-defeating ways, even when they know better? Why do they continue to even after suffering because of it? What if anything more than giving helpful advice and teaching people some behavioral skills can be done about that?

There are two simple answers to the first two questions. First, behavior starts and continues because it serves a purpose. Second, behavior is always goal-orientated. The answer to the third question is to teach the five life skills noted in the introduction.

People would prefer to live as long as they can rather than die prematurely. They would rather be healthy instead of sick, and happy instead of unhappy. People would also prefer to get along with others instead of fight with them, be successful rather than fail, and have as much freedom, and control over their own destiny as possible. Ideally, all their energy and effort would go toward reaching these goals. However, no one does that perfectly, all the time.

People often have "mistaken" goals that get them off-course from getting what they want, and getting closer to where they really want to be in their life. If they cling to these "mistaken" goals for too long, they often lose sight of what the real "prize" once was. For example, family members can have "mistaken" goals that cause them to fight with each other so much that they never get what they really want from each other, and never get to feel the way they want with each other in their family. If they continue to fight and argue, they can gradually lose hope of ever getting what they want, and eventually forget what it was that they once wanted.

Years ago, a man named Rudolf Dreikurs observed children misbehaving in classrooms and postulated that they misbehaved because they had one or more of four "mistaken" goals. Linda Albert wrote a book entitled *A Teacher's Guide to Cooperative Discipline* based on his work. The mistaken goals he identified were:

1) Power and Control; for students to prove to teachers and others that they have the power and are in control instead of others

2) Revenge; to get back at, or get even with teachers and others for a real or perceived transgression

3) Attention; to get the attention, acceptance, approval, or admiration of others

4) Avoidance of Failure; to avoid failing or appearing to fail and reliving feelings like shame and guilt that went with doing so in the past; to avoid the anxiety that comes from expecting to fail when confronted with new challenges

These goals were "mistaken" because in achieving these goals, students sacrificed to a large degree the chance to reach other, more constructive and productive goals they might have had, or could have had, like being successful in school and getting along with teachers.

These "mistaken" goals also explain a great deal of unhealthy, self-defeating behavior of all kinds, in and out of a classroom. For example, young teens often start to smoke at least in part because it is a way to show mom and dad, and authorities of various kinds, that they are going to do whatever they want, and no one could stop them. It is sometimes a way to get back at or get even with parents for a real or perceived transgression because the teen knows, or at least imagines, that their parents will be upset if and when they learn of the teen's smoking. At the same time, it might be a way for teens to believe they are connected to, or have the acceptance and approval of friends who engage in the same behavior.

So many family arguments and disagreements have the "mistaken" goals of power and control, and revenge. Some families get so locked into fighting and arguing that it begs the question, what would they being doing together if they were not fighting and arguing? Sadly, the answer might sometimes be nothing at all. Sometimes, the negative attention that occurs when family members fight and argue seems to be better than none at all for the persons involved.

Another "mistaken goal" that explains so much unhealthy

behavior is what I call Withdrawal-Avoidance-Relief. There are many behaviors, some that are healthy, and many others that are not, that can serve the purpose of helping people temporarily withdraw from, avoid or get relief from unpleasantness in their lives. For example, smoking, drinking, using drugs, and overeating, just to mention a few. Having sex can too, and that is why so many people make mistakes with it. While teens may start smoking with the mistaken goal of power and control, revenge or attention, the reason they keep smoking is usually because they quickly learn that it gives them relief from stress and anxiety, among other things. Getting this temporary relief is "mistaken" because it often quickly leads to the long-term struggle with addiction so often seen in smokers, and subsequent health problems later in life. Smoking is still a major cause of death.

We have had a "drug war" for over three decades. Periodically, questions have arisen about the effectiveness of it and whether the money spent and actions taken have paid off in any appreciable way. There have been periodic successes on the supply side of the problem, in interdicting the movement of drugs into and around this country. However, the demand for illegal drugs has stayed the same or even increased. As long as there continues to be such a huge demand, there will be always be people who are willing to risk and try anything and everything to meet it to make money. This demand is caused by the fact that drugs serve a purpose in so many peoples lives. As long as they do, there will continue to be a demand. The thing that gives drugs purpose in the first place is that people generate a dysfunctional amount of emotion.

A Dysfunctional Amount of Emotion

A large part of what gives rise to "mistaken" goals, and purpose to unhealthy, self-defeating behavior is that people generate a dysfunctional amount of emotion in the form of anger, anxiety, depression, shame and guilt, loneliness, boredom and low frustration tolerance (LFT). Anger, for example, goes hand in hand with the mistaken goals of power and control, and revenge. People are more prone to seek the attention, acceptance, approval or love of others in an irrational, unhealthy and self-defeating way when they feel lonely, or perhaps anxious and depressed. Students, and adults as well, are often likely to have the mistaken goal of avoidance of failure when they feel shame or guilt about past efforts and performances, and generate intense anxiety about future ones because of it. And, people regularly use all types of behavior, some healthy, many not, to temporarily withdraw from or avoid unpleasant circumstances in their lives and to get relief from the anxiety, depression, shame and guilt, loneliness and even boredom that go with those life events.

Emotion is not an inherently bad thing. It was naturally

selected for retention, even in its most intense forms, because it served some survival purpose. In a sense, the problem is that we have a cave-man model for a body, but are trying to live in a much more civilized society. Culture can change must faster than biology. Even in modern life though, there are times when plugging into "fight or flight" might be lifesaving. There are many other times when some e-motion can be helpful "energy to move" to make life better. For example, if a teacher has a day of classes that doesn't go as he or she wanted them to, the frustration he or she feels at the end of the day can motivate him or her to develop a plan overnight so that the next day of classes goes better than the one he or she just had. Without that emotion, the teacher might simply come back the next day and have the same kind of experience. On the other hand, if a teacher were to get angry, he or she could end up reacting instead of responding to a situation he or she did not like, and make a lot of mistakes with his or her students that would only make matters worse. Remember, there are two ways to make something worse, do nothing and overreact to it.

In many modern life situations, the amount of emotion people generate in reaction or response to their life events often ends up being:

1) More than is healthy for them
2) More than they know what to do with
3) More than is helpful or necessary for the situation they find themselves in
4) An amount that works against them instead of for them

Too much emotion of any kind can literally make people sick. It is common to see people stymied and paralyzed because they are overwhelmed by the way they feel. Students often ask Terry London, "Aren't there some times when getting angry is good?" His answer is always that whatever people can do when they are mad, they can do better when they are not. It's also common to see people say and do things while experiencing intense emotions that even they know are not best for them, and that only make their lives worse instead of better.

When the first tape recorder came out they had a lighted dial that had a needle that moved from left to right as the volume of the sound increased. If there were too little volume, there would not be any recording. If there were too much volume, there would be feedback. The volume had to be just right, and the needle had to be somewhere in the middle to get the best recording.

This can be a good visual for helping people see how feelings become dysfunctional. Feelings like frustration, irritation, disappointment, concern, sadness, regret and remorse can help motivate people to make necessary changes in their life. It motivates them, an allows them to respond to their life events, and can therefore be very functional. However, feelings like anger, anxiety, depression, shame, guilt and loneliness end up being dysfunctional more often than not. These emotions cause people to react instead of respond. They often lead to people saying and doing things that make their lives worse instead of better, or people avoiding doing things that might make their lives better. See the diagram that follows.

It's important to note that anger is not just a greater quantity of what frustration is. It is a qualitatively different emotion. It is because of how the two feelings come about. They have different cognitive origins. There can be varying intensities of frustration and anger, but they are not simply stronger or weaker versions of each other. The same is true for sadness and depression, concern and anxiety, shame and regret, guilt and remorse.

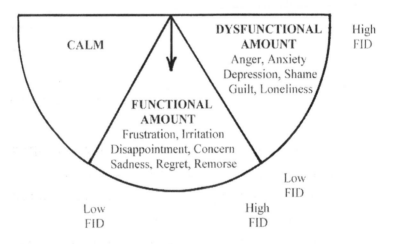

Whenever we talk about feelings such as anger, anxiety, depression, shame, guilt, loneliness, boredom and LFT, there are three parameters we need to look at. They are:

1) F = Frequency
2) I = Intensity
3) D = Duration

It is perfectly understandable for human beings to generate anger, anxiety, depression, shame and guilt, loneliness and even boredom in response to their life situations. A little bit of these now and then may not hurt anything or anyone. The problem is that people generate a higher frequency, intensity and duration of such emotions than is necessary or helpful. Doing so makes people more prone to having "mistaken" goals, and gives more purpose to unhealthy, self-defeating behavior. It also:

1) Causes people to react instead of respond to life events
2) Causes people to act impulsively without thinking things through first
3) Makes it harder for people to access and act on helpful information and advice
4) Makes it harder for people to do what they are capable of doing, to perform skills they have learned
5) Makes it harder for people to learn from their own and others' experiences
6) Makes it less likely that people will consider potential consequences before acting
7) Makes otherwise smart people do stupid things

When the many problems that individuals, families, schools and society face are analyzed, it becomes apparent that most are caused, directly or indirectly, by people generating a greater frequency, intensity and duration of emotion than is necessary or helpful, and what they do because of that, or to deal with it.

That's why emotional management is considered the first and most important life skill people need to learn to be as functional as possible. Unfortunately, families and schools typically do little if anything to really teach young people how to effectively manage their emotions. This is despite the role an inability to do so plays in so much that goes wrong in schools and elsewhere, and at every stage of life. Dispensing consequences does not teach people how to manage their emotions better. It just gives people a reason to stop behaving a certain way. If they were generating too much emotion, they probably would not stop anyway. People who have been punished for what they did while angry, often just get angrier. Though "anger management" has become an everyday word, much of what is done to help people manage their anger better is often ineffective. Some people naturally manage their emotions fairly well. They may or may not be able to tell others how they do it. However, many people do not, and all people, regardless of prior ability or lack of it, and regardless of age, can be taught to do it better.

Here is a life skills model from the book *Rough Spot Training* by Terry London and Amor Monjes. This book is an excellent manual for parents on how to teach elementary age students to begin managing their emotions more effectively. These life skills are listed in order of importance.

1) Emotional Management
2) Self-soothing and regulation
3) Goal formation
4) Problem solving
5) Communication
6) Behavioral skills
7) Literacy and Academic skills

It is easy to see how things can go badly. If people do not manage their emotions effectively, it sets the stage for them trying to sooth or regulate themselves in unhealthy, self-defeating ways, For example, by using things like tobacco, alcohol and drugs, or even eating or having sex, and learning that these things work. That is the problem with such things. They work. They can alter peoples' moods and give them temporary relief.

Most adults who struggle with tobacco, alcohol or drugs started using them early in life. The mistake they made back then was analogous to looking up answers in the back of a math book when problems were assigned for homework. It gave them a quick and easy answer to their problem. They felt better fast, if only temporarily. However, doing so deprived them of the opportunity to learn how to manage their emotions more effectively, and solve everyday problems. That is why so many adults who struggle with tobacco, alcohol and drugs are today no better at managing their emotions and solving their everyday life problems than they were as kids. Part of the problem though is that their families and teachers never really taught them how to manage their emotions effectively, and might even have instead given them plenty of life events that they might understandably have disturbed themselves about.

Please note that Literacy and Academic skills are at the bottom of the list. Many young people have traumatic life events outside the classroom that they understandably struggle to manage their emotional reactions to. Some are naturally resilient, but many others struggle. It sets the stage for them to seek ways to sooth or regulate themselves in unhealthy, self-defeating ways. It also sets the stage for them to have multiple "mistaken" goals. Bottom line, it adversely affects their readiness and willingness to learn.

Now consider the cognitive and emotional toll on young children, who for whatever reason, are always the ones who do not get it when everyone else does. Imagine what they might start to think it means about them and their abilities, and the shame and guilt they might generate because of that. Consider how that might cause them to be overly anxious when presented with future challenges and opportunities, and cause them to have the mistaken goal of avoidance of failure in the classroom, and perhaps withdrawal, avoidance and relief in starting to smoke, drink or use drugs outside it. Many young people generate anger to protect themselves. This only serves to add the mistaken goals of power and control, and revenge to their repertoire. Then birds of a feather flock together and break away from the mainstream. Some of this may happen no matter what adults do, but teaching young people effective emotional management from early on in age appropriate ways sure could not hurt.

Too often in education, teachers try to put the cart before the horse. What the life skills model suggests is that being deficient in emotional management can make functioning in a school setting much more difficult, regardless of how much good teaching takes place or how much academic accommodation students receive.

Here are some quotes from Rough Spot Training that highlight the important role emotional management plays in peoples' lives, in particular their education.

1) "A person's behavior follows his or her emotions toward his or her life events"

2) "If a person cannot manage his or her emotional response to his or her life events, he or she will either make poor behavioral choices, or sabotage his or her performance"

3) "If a person is deficient in the first three life skills, then limit setting, behavior modification, and behavior skills training will have a superficial and short-term effect at best"

UNCONDITIONAL SELF-ACCEPTANCE

The feeling of shame deserves some special discussion. Shame occurs when people believe they do not live up to their own or others' expectations. That might seem to be a helpful feeling to have at some times, but the problem, as Dr. Albert Ellis used to say, is that "shame blocks change". It gets in the way of people taking an objective look at how they think, feel, say and do things, and perhaps seeking help that is available to them to make their life better. It makes them want to deny that something's wrong, and run away from the truth, rather than face it and fix what might need fixing. One of the most common examples would be the denial alcoholics often exhibit. People often think alcoholics really don't get that they have a problem, but symptoms like keeping a hidden stash and sneaking drinks suggest otherwise. They know full well they have a problem, but the intense shame they generate for what they've done to their own lives and the lives of loved ones keeps them acknowledging their mistake, and making the necessary changes in their lives. It also gives them even more reason to drink.

In Rational Emotive Behavioral Therapy, shame is called a secondary disturbance. An REBT therapist is taught to always treat the secondary disturbance first, before attempting to treat the primary disturbance, which might be something like anxiety, or depression. Otherwise, shame will continue to block the change the client needs to make.

The way to keep shame from blocking change that might be helpful or even necessary is to teach people to have USA or Unconditional Self-Acceptance. That can be accomplished by getting people to see, and truly believe, that anything they think, feel, say or do is perfectly understandable. That doesn't mean it's healthy for them, or that others will find it acceptable. It just means that:

1) They will never be the first or last person in human history to think, feel, say or do something a certain way, or to make a certain kind of mistake

2) They have got a lot of company—there are a lot of other people who have thought, felt, said and done the same things, and made the same mistakes, and there will be even more in the future

3) If you put other people through the exact same life experience, more often than not they would probably end up thinking, feeling, saying and doing similar things

4) It is part of being human for people to think, feel, say and do things certain ways when exposed to certain types of life events

5) Given the genetics some people inherited, and the life experiences they have had, many of which they had no control over, they have in some sense done the best they could—they could always have done better, but human beings are not perfect

6) It is nothing to be ashamed of—regret yes, but it won't help for people to beat up on themselves, and it only makes moving forward even harder

7) People are all FHB's, or Fallible Human Beings who at times think, feel, say and do things that make their own and others' lives worse instead of better.

People cannot make others look at themselves this way. If they could, therapy would be much easier and more successful. People can only present this view as one of many ways for others to choose to look at themselves and what happens. It's ultimately their choice how they do.

There are many other things people could say to themselves to help them have USA, especially when things are not going so well. These are called Effective Coping Statements. For example:

Everyone makes mistakes

No one's perfect

Whatever I did was understandable

It's not the end of the world

It could be a lot worse

Others are entitled to make mistakes and so am I

I can only do so much

Whatever I do is good enough

I did the best I could at the time

It won't help to beat up on myself

Anger is another feeling that deserves some special mention. It's typically the hardest feeling to get people to let go of. People will do just about anything to stop feeling anxious, depressed, ashamed, guilty, lonely or bored, and often do. However, they will often cling to their anger. The reasons are:

1) It gives them a false sense of power

2) It gives them a false sense of righteousness (Terry London always asks his students "Ever met an angry person who thought they were wrong?")

3) It gives them a false sense of permission to do things to other people

4) It protects them from feelings other ways that they don't like.

As long as people keep feeling angry, they do not have to feel anxious, depressed, ashamed, guilty, or lonely. People can often be seen slipping into feeling anxious, depressed, ashamed or guilty when they let go of their anger. They will often then protect themselves by injecting themselves with anger much as people might inject themselves with drugs. For example, when confronted with the facts about their drinking, alcoholics will often protect themselves from feeling shame and guilt by getting angry. Teaching and encouraging people to have USA, or Unconditional Self-Acceptance, can help remove any perceived need to do so in alcoholics or anyone else.

LOCUS OF CONTROL

The most important determinant of how effectively people manage their emotions is the type of locus of control they have. The term stands for where people see their feelings as coming from; what they see as the cause of their feelings. People can have an external or internal locus of control.

Most people have an external locus of control. They believe that what others say and do, and what happens makes them feel the way they do. There are some problems with that:

1) People end up feeling worse than necessary or helpful, for longer than necessary

2) People can end up perceiving themselves as victims of their circumstances with no apparent way to feel better. This can lead to helplessness and hopelessness.

3) It implies that others or their life circumstances must change for them to feel better, and they do not control what others think, feel, say or do, and cannot always control everything that happens

4) People miss many opportunities to feel better

Anything that someone else says or does, or that happens, is technically just an event in peoples' lives. People call events all kinds of things: problems, troubles, mistakes, accidents, challenges, and opportunities to name a few. What they choose to call an event does not change what happened. It just makes it easier or harder to deal with. It just causes people to generate more or less emotion. No matter what they choose to call what happens, what others say and do and what happens is still just an event.

Formulas can be written for the way people see their feelings arising and what they see as the cause of them. If people have an external locus of control, the formula would be something like the following:

$$Events = Feelings$$

They believe the event actually causes their feeling. If asked why, they typically say "Because I wouldn't have felt that way if it hadn't happened". There might be some truth to that. That's why, as you'll learn later, Dr. Ellis called such events Activating vents. However, most people at some time have gotten all upset about something they thought happened, only to later learn that it never did. They have also gotten upset about things they imagined would happen, but probably never would. People do not have to have real events occur for them to get upset. People can upset themselves about imagined events just as much as they can about real ones. A second reason people believe their life events cause their feelings is because there is usually so little time between something happening and the way they feel that they cannot imagine that there is anything in between. They cannot imagine any intervening variable. The third reason is that most everyone else seems to look at things that way, and believe that. Most people believe that what others say and do, and what happens, makes them feel the way they do. Most people have an external locus of control.

The real formula for feelings is:

$$Events + Thoughts = Feelings$$

Thoughts cause feelings, not events. It is just like that first algebraic equation everyone gets:

$$a + b = c$$

Where a is a constant, and b is a variable. If a stays the same and you change b, c changes too. Likewise, if an event stays the same, and people change their thoughts about it, their feeling changes. Sometimes it changes for the better, other times for the worse.

Life is full of examples to demonstrate this. So many times, two people react with completely different emotions, or different intensities and duration of the same emotion, to the same event. Even at funerals, there are times when people are crying, times when they are laughing, and other times when they are just sad, or even comforted to some degree. The event, the death of a significant person in their lives, does not change. However, what they are thinking at any given moment does. And, as time goes by, time heals for most people largely because they think about the loss of a significant person in their lives less, or adopt some ways of thinking about the loss that allows them to better tolerate it. Of course, some do not, and continue to struggle with their loss.

I believe that at some level most people already do know that it is the way they think that really causes how they feel, and not the events of their lives. I used to give my students a worksheet with twenty pairs of thoughts and I would ask them to select the thought that they believed would make people angrier. The vast, vast majority of students were able to pick all twenty thoughts correctly. That always suggested to me that they already knew that thinking one way could make people feel better or worse than thinking another way. It was as if they saw the true relationship between thoughts and feelings, but the picture was fuzzy. All they needed was for me to bring it into focus for them. All they needed was for someone to point it out to them. Unfortunately, their parents and other teachers had not. I was in my late thirties before my friend Jerry Rankin first pointed it out to me. Personally, I think it is sad that we teach young people so much about life around them and how it works, but largely neglect to teach them one of the most basic, but important relationships there is. That thoughts cause feelings, not events.

It is actually a good thing that thoughts cause feelings, and not events. It means people can exercise more control over how they end up feeling than most people realize. The thoughts people generate in response to life events are more often than not automatic. They are the product of much rehearsal and practice, and therefore well "rutted" in peoples' brains. That is why people often believe they are at the mercy of their life events and have no real control over how they feel, or power to change it. However, the thoughts they generate are not cast in stone. People can learn to think differently in response to life events.

Locus of Control

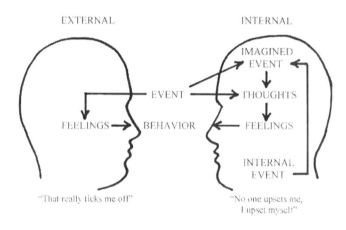

COGNITIVE CHOICES

People have a host of cognitive choices that they make all the time, usually automatically, and without being fully aware that they do. For example:

1) How they look at things
2) What meaning they attach to what happens
3) What they focus on
4) What they compare things, themselves and their life to
5) What they expect of ourselves, others and life
6) What they imagine will happen next
7) How much importance they attach to what happens

There is always more than one way to look at anything that happens. There is always more than one meaning people could attach to what happens. There is always more than one thing people can focus on. For example, people could focus on what they have, or what they do not have. They can focus what they believe is going right, or what they think is going wrong. They can focus on what they like about what they see in the mirror, or what they do not. There are also many different people and situations that they could use for comparisons. People could compare themselves to some and feel wealthy, lucky, and smart, and compare themselves to others and feel the opposite. People can expect just about anything they want of themselves, others and life, from way too much to perhaps too little. They can imagine all kinds of things happening before anything actually does, from something really wonderful to something really horrible. What people imagine may have little or no effect on what actually transpires, and little or no resemblance to it. People can also attach varying degrees of importance to anything that happens. They can treat it as a really big deal, something really insignificant, or anything in between.

The way most people make such cognitive choices is typically automatic because they have rehearsed and practiced the way they do so many times in the past. They have also seen and heard others do so from early in their lives on. That is why they are often unaware that they have any choice in the matter. However, people always do have a choice because they could have looked at things another way or attached a different meaning to what happened. They could have focused on something else. They could have compared things to something else. They could have expected something different of themselves, others and life, and imagined something different happening before hand. They also could have made a bigger or smaller deal of something than they did.

The way people make such choices may be understandable given their history. It may also be automatic because of sheer repetition and rehearsal. However, the way they do is not cast in stone. People can learn to make these cognitive choices differently, and better. The first step toward doing so is for them to recognize that they do have such choices.

So what is the best way for people to make such choices? It often depends on the situation. The key question is, does it make people feel better or worse to think certain ways? And, does it help or do them any good to feel bad? Most importantly, does thinking the way they do make them want to keep going, and try harder, or give up? That is the real test. So much of what goes right in life is the product being patient and persevering.

There are some simple but important questions people can and should ask themselves and others along these lines.

1) What do I (you) really want? (How would I (you) really like to feel?)
2) Does the way I (you) think, and feel, say and do things get me (you) what I (you) really want?
3) Will it make it easier or harder to get what I (you) really want in the future if I (you) continue to think, and feel, say and do things the way I (you) always have?
4) Does it make my (your) life better or worse to think, and feel, say and do things that way?
5) How is it working for me (you) to think, and feel, say and do things the way I (you) currently do?
6) If someone else thinks, and feels, says and does things that way, am (are) I (you) likely to get what I (you) really want with them, or from them if they continue to?

A few years back, a friend went through a divorce. He didn't see it coming. The way his ex-wife handled it was not very nice. He would routinely call me and be extremely distraught, with periodic fits of anger that gave rise to talk of acts of retribution, most of which would have violated all kinds of laws and only made his life much worse. I would do my best job of listening, and active listening, helping him verbalize and clarify for him and me how he was looking at things. What he thought it all meant, what he was focusing on, comparing things to, and imagining. At some point, I would quietly ask him, "So how's it working for you to think and look at things that way?" There would always be a long pause of silence, followed by a soft "Not very well". Then I would tactfully explain to him that we all have choices as to how we want to look at things, choices that we alone can make. The way he was looking at things was perfectly understandable given what had happened, and I told him so. I might have looked at things the same way if it had happened to me. However, there are always emotional consequences, good or bad, or something in between, for whatever way people choose to look at things. And, there were other ways to look at things at the time that might have made him feel better, or at least not as bad. I brainstormed some of those for him, but I couldn't make him look at things those ways. It was his choice. I tried to repeatedly remind him that if you can't make something better, at least don't make it worse.

At the time we talked, his ex-wife had already returned to

her ex-husband in Florida. It was perfectly understandable that my friend got upset about what she did, and even that he saw her as the cause of his feelings. Most other people would do the same, and people do it all the time. The problem with looking at things the way he did was that it gave her seeming power and control over how he felt, even when she was 1500 miles away and no longer part of his life. It did not make sense to give someone who had so wronged him that much seeming power and control over how he felt, especially when she was not even anywhere near. Furthermore, she was down in Florida having a great time reuniting with her ex-husband. He had no trouble envisioning exactly how. It did not make sense for my friend to feel bad while they were enjoying life, when he had done nothing but treat her nicely, and she was the one who really did something inappropriate. I tried to convince him that the best way to get even was to live well.

When I was a teacher, if I had gotten really upset anytime a student said something I did not like, and I had believed that they made me mad, it would have given my students seeming power and control over how I felt. If they believed they could make me mad anytime they wanted to, some probably would have said and done things more often, even if they suffered consequences, just because it would have given them a false sense of power. And, if I had gone home at night and continued to be upset about what they said or did earlier in the day, they would not have been doing that to me, I would have been. They would not have been there, and what they said or did occurred hours earlier. Furthermore, if they went home at night and had fun playing video games, it would not have made any sense for me to stomp around the house all night, screaming at my wife and daughter for little things, and kicking the dog because I was still angry about what a student had said or done during the day.

People like to have as much power and control over their own live as possible. That is what this is all about. It is about power and control. When people see what others say and do, and what happens as the cause of how they feel, it is understandable. However, they needlessly give others and events they often cannot control seeming power that those people and events really do not have. They give away power and control they do have, usually without realizing that they do. Real power is not getting mad and yelling, flipping people off, or punching them out whenever they say or do things we do not like. Real power is choosing if and when we are going to get upset instead of putting our emotions at the mercy of others and events. Real power is choosing how upset we are going to get, and how long we are going to stay upset.

Picture an argument between two people, with one screaming and yelling at the top of their voice, and the other calmly responding to questions but otherwise not saying much at all. Who is in control? Picture two children, with one being angry and calling the other every type of name they can. The second child is smiling and just keeps saying, "I know you are, but what am I?". Every time they do, the first child just gets even angrier. Who is in control? Who has the power?

If people want to free themselves to stop behaving in unhealthy, self-defeating ways, and to make better choices and act in their best interest, they need to reduce the purpose served in behaving in their old ways. To do that, they need to learn to generate a more functional amount of emotion in response to their life events. They need to learn how to get better, rather than continue to rely on things outside themselves to just temporarily feel better. The most important step they can take toward doing so is to develop an internal locus of control. They do that by first learning and remembering the true cause of their feelings; that their thoughts cause how they feel, not the events of their lives. Second, it will help for them to learn and remember the cognitive choices they and others always have. Third, they need to learn how to use this new knowledge to their advantage, and practice doing so as much as possible. Becoming proficient at doing so is extremely empowering. It will give them a greater sense of power and control over their emotional and behavioral destiny. It will help them learn to keep the power and control they do have, rather than continue to give it away without realizing it, as people so often do.

When I was young, one of the popular comedians at the time used to say, "I went to the doctor and said doc it hurts when I do this. My doctor said, then stop doing that". I am not sure why that was funny back then, but the same thing applies here. If people feel worse when they think a certain way, it would seem obvious that the solution would be to stop thinking that way and start rehearsing thinking some new way.

I make regular trips across the country. When my daughter was at the University of North Carolina, I would travel from Chicago to Asheville just about every other week. I love to vacation in and photograph the desert Southwest, so I have made many trips to Utah, Arizona and Nevada. There is something happening on the public air waves that concerns me, and I believe should concern others too.

Without most people being aware of it, a relatively small number of large media corporations have bought up the vast majority of major radio stations across the country, especially those with the strongest signals that cover the largest areas. These stations carry the same nationally syndicated talk show hosts daily. Some of these hosts are on 600 stations every day. There is always more than one way to look at anything. However, what these hosts typically do is to select only one of the many ways of looking at things, and present it as the only viable one. They then misrepresent other points of view rather than allowing political or ideological opponents to present their points of view for themselves. There often seems to be such a coordination between the different talk show hosts during the day that the phrase "talking points" has become commonplace. These nationally syndicated hosts then repeat and reiterate their selected points of view day after day, week after week.

In the next chapter, cognitive, emotional and behavioral "ruts" are discussed. Basically, if someone thinks, feels, says or does something over and over again, or sees and hears others do so, they develop "ruts" in their brains. The thoughts, feelings and behaviors these "ruts" give rise to then become automatic. When the way people look at things becomes "rutted" and automatic, mere opinions can take on the credibility of facts. The line gets blurred.

The American Heritage on-line definition of propaganda is: The systematic propagation of a doctrine or cause or of information reflecting the views and interests of those advocating such a doctrine or cause. The Wikipedia definition is: Propaganda is the dissemination of information aimed at influencing the opinions or behaviors of people. As opposed to impartially providing information, propaganda in its most basic sense, often presents information primarily in order to influence its audience. Propaganda often presents facts selectively (thus lying by omission) to encourage a particular synthesis, or gives loaded messages in order to produce an emotional rather than rational response to the information presented. The desired result is a change of the attitude toward the subject in the target audience to further a political agenda. Dictionary.com says that propaganda is information, ideas, or rumors deliberately spread widely to help or harm a person, group, movement, institution, nation, etc; the particular doctrines or principles propagated by an organization or movement.

As school children, we were taught that the Soviet Union had state run media, and that it broadcast propaganda daily to its citizens to brainwash them. We were encouraged to look down our noses at such a practice because it was so un-American. We were a country of free speech and free thinkers. As I drive across the country, I cannot help but wonder how what we have in America since the Fairness Doctrine was eliminated is any different, except that it is corporate owned, determined and run instead of state. It's not healthy for people, and definitely not healthy for the country. Sadly, many people around the country proudly call themselves "ditto heads".

These same nationally syndicated talk radio hosts are now telling their audiences that the federal government is going to try to target them and quiet them by re-instituting the Fairness Doctrine. They say it would be a violation of free speech. That's one way to look at it. However, the speech of these talk show hosts is anything but free. The richest corporations buy the most, and the biggest stations and then dictate the programming that audiences have to choose from. They pay these hosts hundreds of millions of dollars to do what they do best. They are no longer required by law to present any opposing views in their programming.

WHY IT'S HARD TO CHANGE

Everything people think, feel, say or do is the product of connections or pathways that develop over time between nerve cells in their brains. When people rehearse or practice thinking, feeling, saying or doing something a certain way, what happens in their brain tissue is analogous to what happens when people walk the same path over and over again in a field or forest. They create "ruts" in their brains to think, feel, say or do something. Once these "ruts" are created, it becomes automatic to think, feel, say or do those particular things. That could be helpful in some instances, but it often ends up being quite the opposite. When people have ruts for thoughts that make them feel worse than they need to, and cause them to behave in ways that make their life worse instead of better, Dr. Ellis called those thoughts "automatic irrational beliefs". Much of what goes wrong in the lives of individuals, families, schools and society as a whole results from people slipping into their cognitive, emotional and behavioral "ruts", in particular those for their "automatic irrational beliefs" about themselves, others, and life.

The problem people face if and when they try to change the

way they think, feel, say or do things is that once these connections and pathways are made between their nerve cells, they cannot be broken in any way short of trauma to the brain. Once people create these "ruts" in their brains to think, feel, say and do things a certain way, they cannot get rid of them. They can only make new ones. In order for a new way of thinking, feeling, saying and doing things to compete with their old automatic ways, people need to first make a new connection or pathway for thinking, feeling, saying and doing something different. Then, they need to practice and rehearse that new way so that the new pathway that gives rise to it becomes "rutted" and it can compete with the old way. It is that simple, and that tough.

This simple way of viewing brain physiology can partly explain why people keep making the same mistakes, even when they know better. It is part of the reason why people can stop smoking for years, have one cigarette, and be back to smoking two packs a day in no time at all. It is probably why people say, "Once an alcoholic, always an alcoholic" and other similar things. It is why people can and should expect to revert at any time to their old ways of thinking, feeling, saying and doing things. The question is always whether they are going to plug into their old ruts, or perhaps newer, healthier, and more constructive ones.

NEW WAYS TO TALK ABOUT FEELINGS

In English classes, if students misspeak or write in semantically or grammatically incorrect ways, their teachers will usually be quick to correct them. This even happens in everyday life. However, people routinely misspeak about the origin or cause of their feelings, and no one says anything. Families, schools, churches and other parts of society do little if anything to really teach or encourage people to have an internal locus of control. Actually, all these institutions, radio and TV personalities, and popular music do quite the opposite. The way people talk gives others a good idea as to how they really look at things. If people listen to the way they and the vast majority of others talk about their feelings, the way radio and TV personalities do, or even the way popular music artists do in their songs, they will note that the vast majority of people have an external locus of control and most probably do not even realize it. The vast majority of people everywhere talk as if what others say and do, and what happens is really the cause of how they feel.

There are more semantically correct and precise ways of

talking about feelings. All people really need to do is attach "It's my choice…" to the cognitive choices noted above. For example:

It's my (your) choice how I (you) look at things

It's my (your) choice what meaning I (you) attach to what happens

It's my (your) choice what I (you) focus on

It's my (your) choice what I (you) compare things to

It's my (your) choice what I expect of myself (yourself), others and life

It's my (your) choice what I (you) imagine will happen next

It's my (your) choice how much importance I (you) attach to what happens

And, since the way people choose to think about what happens determines how they feel, it is logically also true that:

It's my (your) choice how I (you) want to feel

These new ways of talking remind people of the choices they have, and that they make them all the time without realizing it. They also remind people that they have more power and control over how they feel than they usually realize or give themselves credit for. Finally, these statements remind people that they often give away the real power and control that they do have to others and life events, both of which they often have little if any real control over.

Unfortunately, people often misinterpret what someone means the first time they hear someone tell them that it's their choice how they want to feel. I know I did, and many of my students did too. People often think others are saying:

    a) It is their fault they feel the way they do

    b) There is something wrong with them for feeling the way they do

They also might think someone is discounting or minimizing how important the event in question is to their lives. People who have recently lost significant loved ones often think that. Last, they might wrongly think someone is excusing other peoples' behavior. They often react with, "So you're saying it's OK that they did that to me?"

That's why it is important to remind people that anything they feel, or think, say and do is perfectly understandable. However, there will be emotional consequences for thinking certain ways, whether it is understandable or not. Furthermore, people can exercise more control over how they feel than they might ever have realized. The only thing that is worse than others saying and doing things is for people to continue to upset themselves long after the fact, especially when no amount of emotion will ever change what has happened. It would be even worse if others would get to enjoy seeing people upset themselves, and believe they caused it.

Here is another way to look at it. One person says or does something, and a second person gets all upset. The first person moves on and forgets all about what he or she said or did. The second person stays upset for a long time. Who wins? Now suppose that first person wanted the second person to get and stay upset to get even for some real or perceived transgression. Who really wins?

When my mother died, I would never have gone up to my father while he was sobbing at her casket and said, "Dad, it's your choice how you want to feel". My father was never big on showing emotion, and I could sense he did not like to cry in front of people. I told him at every opportunity that whatever he thought and felt at a time like that was perfectly understandable. When my brother called me a few days after the funeral because he was upset that our father had started smoking again, I told him that was also understandable. It certainly was not healthy, and his concern was also understandable, and I shared it. However, smoking (and drinking) had served a purpose in our father's life since he was a 17 year-old infantryman and severely wounded in WWII. Now he had lost the woman he had spent over 50 years with. He was doing the only thing he knew how to do when overwhelmed with emotion. At least he did not start drinking again. On the other hand, if months later, my dad had still been severely depressed, it might have been time to start tactfully talking to him about how he was choosing to look at things. However, I would have tempered my effort with the knowledge that even if he were looking at things in a way that depressed him needlessly, and even threatened his health, it too would unfortunately have been understandable. And, ultimately, it would have been his choice alone to make as to how he wanted to look at what happened from that day forward.

There are other new, and more semantically correct and helpful ways people could start talking about their feelings. For example:

No one upsets me (you), I (you) upset myself (yourself)

They don't make me (you) mad, I (you) do

I (you) upset myself when that happens

I'm (you're) disturbing myself (yourself) about that

I'm (You're) responsible for how I (you) feel, not others

They're not responsible for how I (you) feel, I am (you are)

It's not their job to make me (you) feel better, it's mine (yours)

It's my (your) job to make myself (yourself) feel better, not theirs

No one can make me (you) happy, only I (you) can

It's not their problem if I (you) feel bad, it's mine (yours)

It's my (your) problem if I (you) feel bad, not theirs

So how can people start looking at things these new ways? They have to practice and rehearse these new ways of thinking and talking. There is no shortcut. It takes a good deal of practice and rehearsal to create some new "ruts" for looking at things these new ways. However, no matter how much practice and rehearsal people do, they can still, at any time, slip back into their old "ruts" and say things like "That really makes me mad". I still do after years of teaching such things. In fact, it is perfectly normal and expected to do so. The difference is that people can learn to catch themselves going down their old paths before they get too far and go back and start over.

It is also important for people to avoid taking unnecessary responsibility for how others make themselves feel. Otherwise, it could be used against them. For example, if a young girl thought she made her boyfriend mad by refusing to have sex, he might threaten to end their relationship to get his way, and it might work. Or, people feel a need to defend themselves and can just make an already bad situation worse by what they say and do in the process of doing so. So many arguments that escalate out of control are about whom is to blame, who is at fault. To avoid taking unnecessary responsibility for how others make themselves feel, people need simply change the pronouns in the statements above. For example:

It's their choice how they look at things
It's their choice what they focus on
It's their choice what they compare it to
It's their choice what they want to expect
It's their choice what they imagine
It's their choice how they want to feel
No one upsets them, they upset themselves
Whatever I say or do is just an event for them
I don't make them mad, they do
They're disturbing themselves about that
They're responsible for how they feel, not me

No one can make them happy, only they can
It's not my job to make them feel better, it's theirs
It's not my problem they feel bad, it's theirs

Perception Is Reality?

There is an old saying that "Perception is reality". It does not mean that perception IS reality. It just means that people often believe that the way they perceive reality is in fact reality.

This is important to talk about because the greater the difference between peoples' perceptions and reality, the more emotion they will generate needlessly, and the poorer mental health, and perhaps even social and physical health they will enjoy. To a large extent, mental illness is defined by the degree to which peoples' perceptions differ from reality. It is perfectly understandable, and perhaps even healthy and protective, to imagine something bad happening and to be concerned that it might. However, if the frequency, intensity and duration of those imaginations become too great, people might develop an anxiety disorder, and be considered neurotic. People who regularly see and hear things that aren't really there might be diagnosed as being psychotic. On the contrary, the closer peoples' perceptions are to reality, the better mental, social and physical health they'll enjoy. With that in mind, consider the following questions.

1) Do we make each other mad?
2) Can we make someone else happy? Can they make us happy?
3) Can we make others feel better about themselves? Can they make us feel better about ourselves?
4) Can you hurt someone else's feelings? Can they hurt yours?
5) Do jobs stress people out, or do people stress themselves out?
6) Does "peer pressure" and other types of "pressure" say they're under come from outside someone or inside them?
7) Can someone make another person feel guilty?
8) Can a young person make their parents or coaches proud of them, as they are so often told to do?
9) Do teachers bore students, or do students bore themselves?
10) Can we make someone else feel good sexually, and can they do the same for us?

There are many problems that arise from people thinking that others and events make them angry, hurt their feelings, put pressure on them, and make them feel guilty, or bad about themselves. There are also problems that can and often do result from people believing that they not only can, but also should make others happy. Job stress is a common precursor to a variety of problems, including health problems. Boredom is a common reason students give for not engaging as much as they could in what teachers ask them to do. It is even a reason why teens engage in all manner of risky behavior. People might do some things they find personally undesirable and unacceptable because they not only think they can, but should be able to make someone else feel good sexually, or vice versa. That is why it is important to ponder the questions above.

If people ask an abusive husband and father why he abuses his wife and children, he will probably say it is because they make him mad. Sadly, they will often accept the blame and agree with his reasoning. Anger is generated in a very small area in a deep portion of the brain. If a line is drawn between the two ear canals, and another from between the eyes straight back, where the two intersect is approximately where anger is generated. So how does what one person says or does get inside another person's head and stimulate that deep part of their brain? The answer is it does not. It's semantically and physiologically incorrect to say one person makes another mad.

Have you ever tried to make someone happy and they did not end up that way, or even got upset with you for trying? Have you ever tried to make someone feel better about him or herself, and he or she refused to? Ever do a lot, and give something your best effort, hoping someone would say they are proud of you, and they never did? Most people have had such experiences. If people could truly make someone else happy, or make someone else feel better about him or herself, or pride when they wanted them to, then why can people not do it all the time? It's because they really cannot. People have a choice whether they end up feeling happy, good about themselves or proud. It is not up to others. Abraham Lincoln said, "A man is about as happy as he makes up his mind to be". The same is true for every other feeling.

It is a common mistake for people to make how they feel about themselves, and their self-worth depend too much on what others say and do, and what happens. People have no control over what others say and do, and cannot always control what happens. Others can say and do whatever they want to, and sometimes will even intentionally try to make people feel bad. Things can go badly no matter how hard people try, or how well they do something, especially when other people are involved. That is why it is important to have USA, or Unconditional Self-Acceptance for those times when things don't go as planned, or as people would like. No matter what others say and do, and no matter what happens, people ultimately have a choice as to how they want to look at things, what meaning they want to attach to what happens, what they want to focus on and compare things to, and how much importance they want to attach to what does happen.

Anything one person says or does is simply an event for another. Events do not make people mad. They do not make people feel happy or better about themselves, or proud. It's what people choose to think about the events that does, or does not. It is how they make the cognitive choices noted earlier, that they alone can make. People like to think they can make others happy and feel better because it gives them a sense of power and control, and of importance in the lives of others. However, it is an illusion, and there are some serious things that occur because people mistakenly believe such things.

For the same reason, people can't make someone else feel guilty, or pressured. And jobs don't stress people out. People stress themselves out. It is understandable if people do end up feeling guilty, pressured or stressed out, but it is what people think that does it, not what others say or do, or what happens. Some people could love and look forward to the same job that others despise and dread. If it were really just their jobs, all people doing the same jobs would feel the same level of stress or disdain. Obviously, that's not the way it is. As long as people think it is their jobs and not really the way they choose to look at those jobs, they will be blind to opportunities and ways to reduce their stress and feel better.

Have you ever seen a feeling? Not what someone looks like or acts like when they experience a feeling, but an actual feeling? Have you ever held a feeling in your hand? If people cannot see feelings or hold feelings in their hands, how can they hurt other peoples' feelings, or others hurt theirs? The answer is that people do not and cannot hurt others' feelings. It would be semantically more precise and correct to say that sometimes, when others say and do things people do not like, they might understandably feel what human beings call hurt. This is especially true if the others are people they like, and more importantly, want to like them back. It gets even worse if they not only want others to like them, but think they need for others to. However, people cannot hurt a feeling. And, it is still what people think about what others say or do that causes any hurt, not what the others say or do. If for example, people said, "How could they say something like that? That is an awful thing to say to a friend", they would feel hurt. If instead they said and truly believed, "They're just kidding", they would not feel hurt, even if the other persons were not kidding.

And it is what people think about someone else and how much importance they attach to what the other person says and does that creates pressure, not what the other person actually says or does. If people do not care about someone else, or even do not like them, they probably would not feel any pressure to do what the other person wants. However, if the other person were someone they wanted to like them, they probably would feel some pressure to do what the other person wanted. And, if they not only wanted the other person to like them, but also thought they needed for them to, the pressure will be even greater. Pressure does not come from outside, it comes from inside. It does not come from what others say and do. It comes from what people think about what others say and do, and their relationship to them.

Unfortunately, people often perceive pressure, including

"peer pressure", as something that comes from outside. Teachers and other helping professionals try to teach students and clients to defend against it as if it does. That is why what students and others are taught often does little good. The real underlying causes of pressure are not being acknowledged and targeted. The real underlying cause is what people think about the other persons involved and their relationship with them. And, they can exasperate any pressure they might feel by mistakenly thinking they need for that person to like or love them rather than simply want them to.

There is an old saying, "Beauty is in the eye of the beholder". It means that two people could look at the same things and one might find it beautiful and the other might find it ugly because of the way they each chose to look at the same thing. If beauty is in the eye of the beholder, where is boredom? It is in the same place, the "eye of the beholder".

It is perfectly understandable in this day and age, with all the ways young people have been stimulated with movies, videos games and amusement park rides, that they might find many everyday events boring. This is especially true since people develop a tolerance for stimulation like they do for everything else. Over time it takes more stimulation to get the same rise out of them as before. However, teachers, and school activities don't bore young people. What teachers say and do, and ask students to do, are just events. Technically, students bore themselves by how they choose to look at things. They do it by what they choose to expect in the first place, and what they focus on and compare things to after the fact. Given what their life experiences have been, it is perfectly understandable that they might look at things the way they do, and get bored. However, if young people wait around for others to do something new and exciting for them to not be bored anymore, they may be bored a lot. Generating boredom can also give purpose to all types of risk-taking behavior, including crime, drug use and risky sex. Teachers would do them a service by pointing out, "We don't bore you, you bore yourself" and explaining why that is true.

Adults are always concerned about their sons and daughter having sex before they're married and getting pregnant or contracting an STD. Based on what I have heard and seen while teaching health education for thirty-three years, I cannot help but think some of the behavior we see, especially in guys, is designed to get some practice in so they will know what to do later, and be good at what they do. To the extent that my observation is accurate, such behavior is largely driven by the belief that people can, and should know how to make someone else feel good sexually. The increased availability of pornography probably only makes young guys more likely to think that is true.

People know that there are parts of male and female bodies that have a lot of nerves that if stimulated, can produce sexual arousal, and perhaps even an orgasm. But suppose a strange man walked up to a strange woman on the street and started touching those areas. Would she appreciate it or enjoy it? Probably not. However, if her boyfriend or husband did the same exact thing, she might get a great deal of pleasure from it. It is really what she thinks about who is doing it, and what they are doing that makes a difference. How people feel about themselves also plays an important role in how they end up feeling sexually. The more comfortable people are with their own body images, and in their own skins, the more likely they are to enjoy themselves, or vice versa. Anything people do to or with others sexually is just an event. The other people have to decide whether that is a good or bad thing. That is why the brain is the biggest and most important sex organ in the body.

THE SERENITY POEM

When people learn the real cause of their feelings, the cognitive choices they have, and to use that knowledge to their advantage to feel better, it is called developing an internal locus of control. Another part of developing an internal locus of control is for people to learn to recognize, focus on, and to control what they really have control over, instead of focusing on and trying to control things they cannot.

The Serenity Poem, or Prayer, is something used in many treatment programs and it is something that is often found on posters and cards.

> Give me courage to change things I can
>
> Serenity to accept thing I can't change
>
> And the wisdom to know the difference

The last part is what people typically struggle with, especially in disagreements with others.

Here is a simple way to see which is which. Anything one person says or does is just an event to someone else. The other person will then generate thoughts about what the first person said or did. These thoughts will probably be automatic irrational beliefs he or she has rehearsed and practiced many times in the past. For example, "How dare you say that? You can't talk to me like that." Thoughts like these will cause the second person to generate anger. The second person will then probably say or do something that becomes a new event for the first person. The first person will then generate automatic irrational beliefs about that. That will cause the first person to get angry, and he or she will probably say or do something back. And away we go! See the diagram below

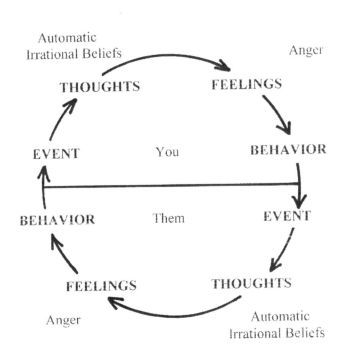

One simple but important question when you look at the circle is which half do you have control over? Whenever I drew this diagram on the chalkboard, and asked this question, there was always an "ah-ah" expression on all my students' faces, and they always immediately knew the right answer. The answer is, only your half. And, which half do most people spend most of their time, energy and effort trying to control? They spend most of it trying to control someone else's half, what someone else thinks, feels, says and does. That is why so much of what people say and do so often does not work the way they intend it to.

Here are some important points to remember:
1) We do not control what others think, feel, say or do
2) We only control what we think, feel, say or do
3) The best we can hope to do is influence what others think, feel, say and do
4) We spend too much time trying to change things we cannot
5) We spend too little time trying to change things we can
6) We spend too much time trying to change what others think, feel, say and do
7) We spend too little time trying to change what we think, feel, say and do
8) The more we try to control what others think, feel, say and do, the more out of control our life feels
9) The more we try to control what others think, feel, say

and do, the more likely they are to have the mistaken goal of power and control, or perhaps even revenge, and think, feel, say and do the opposite. This is especially true with teenagers.

10) The more we focus on controlling what we think, feel, say and do, the more in control we feel

Developing an internal locus of control is one of the most important steps people need to take to truly get better and not just temporarily feel better; to start generating a lower frequency, intensity and duration of emotions like anger, anxiety, depression, shame, guilt, and loneliness. As noted above, learning the real cause of feelings, what the cognitive choices people have are, and to use that new knowledge to feel better is part of what is meant by developing an internal locus of control. Another part is for people to learn to recognize, focus on and to control what they really have control over, and that is what they think, feel, say and do, and not what others do.

This type of education is missing from the education our young people now receive. Teaching and encouraging young people to develop an internal locus of control would not require any new teachers, classes or money. It would be one of the cheapest, quickest and most effective ways to really empower them, and address one of the major underlying causes of so much that goes wrong in the lives of individuals, families and schools and our society as a whole; the fact that people too often generate more emotion than is necessary or helpful. And the best way to start doing that would be to teach and encourage teachers, both current and prospective ones, to develop an internal locus of control for their own good, and the good of their students and own families. Then, ask them to use every possible "teachable moment" to teach and encourage young people to develop an internal locus of control, in a way that's appropriate for the age of their students, and the class they teach.

This would probably be a good time to share some simple rules that can serve as coping statements and help guide people toward making better behavioral choices.

1) If you think, feel, say and do what you have always done, you will get what you have always gotten. Think, feel, say or do something different

2) There are two ways to make a situation worse, do nothing and overreact to it

3) If you cannot make something better, at least don't make it worse

4) Sometimes the best thing to say and do is nothing

Too often, people keep thinking, feeling, saying and doing things the same way and expect different results. Doing so has even been called insanity. Too often people react instead of respond to situations, and often even overreact, because they generate a dysfunctional amount of emotion. Too often people do make situations worse because they generate a dysfunctional amount of emotion and/or think they have to do something.

It might also be a good time to share a simple paradigm developed by an REBT therapist named Dr. Paul Hauck. Dr. Hauck has authored many easy to understand, but extremely informative books on a wide range of emotional and relationship issues. He says that whenever people do not like what is happening to them or the situation they find themselves in, they have three basic healthy options.

1) Problem solve and assert yourself
2) Tolerate what happened without disturbance
3) Leave (the situation, relationship, job)

It really is that simple. Unfortunately, people often aggress against others either verbally or physically instead of asserting themselves. They often tolerate with disturbance. For example, women of all ages unfortunately often tolerated bad behavior from the boys and men in their lives, and do so with emotional disturbance. It is important to remember that people cannot control what others think, feel, say or do. However, it is also important to remember that people get what they tolerate. If people tolerate others bad behavior, with or without disturbance, it might help to ask themselves, "What reason does the other person have to change?"

FEELING BETTER VS. GETTING BETTER

There are many ways to temporarily feel better. Some are healthy, and many are not. Venting is often seen as a healthy way to deal with feelings. It's a major strategy in many programs that involve talk therapy in some form. However, venting is like people blowing their noses when they have a cold. They temporarily can breath better, but their noses quickly start to plug back up because the cause of their congestion and runny nose, a virus, is still infecting their nasal passages. When people vent, they temporarily feel some relief, but their feelings will typically return soon afterward because they return to thinking the way they did before, especially if the same life events continue to present themselves. The cause of their feelings, the automatic irrational beliefs they have about others, life and themselves, and what might have transpired, are still there. They may even have inadvertently been rehearsed again in the process of venting.

Getting better means reducing the overall frequency, intensity and duration of troublesome emotions like anger, anxiety, depression, shame, guilt and loneliness. The only real way to get better is for people to change the way they think, and practice and rehearse the new ways of thinking until those new ways become "rutted" and as automatic as the old ways.

Most people believe that venting anger is better for your health than keeping it in. However, things are not always as they might seem, despite what our common sense might tell us. When this hypothesis was tested, there was no real difference in the number or degree of health problems between those who vented their anger and those who kept it in. The only people who fared better health-wise were those who generated a lower frequency, intensity and duration of anger in the first place.

Behavior Is Just the Tip of the Iceberg

Teachers and parents are rightfully concerned about many behaviors they see in young people. They typically see such behaviors as problems, and then try to reduce or eliminate those behaviors with advice, and more often than not with limit setting and consequences. Society at large does basically the same thing. This often results in spotty success at best.

Behavior is as much a symptom as it is a problem. It is a symptom of much deeper issues that need to be addressed that typically are not. Those deeper issues are the automatic irrational beliefs people have in response to their life events and the feelings and "mistaken" goals those beliefs give rise to.

Behavior is like the symptoms of a cold. People can take OTC medications to temporarily relieve the symptoms, but the symptoms will keep returning when the medications wear off until their bodies eventually fight off the viruses that infect them. Limit setting and consequences are like the OTC medications. They can sometimes temporarily suppress unacceptable behavior. The automatic irrational beliefs are like the viruses. They are the underlying cause of the behavior. Attitude is always the father of behavior. When behavior doesn't change, even in the face of harsh consequences, it is typically because the underlying attitudes that father it, and give purpose to it, have not.

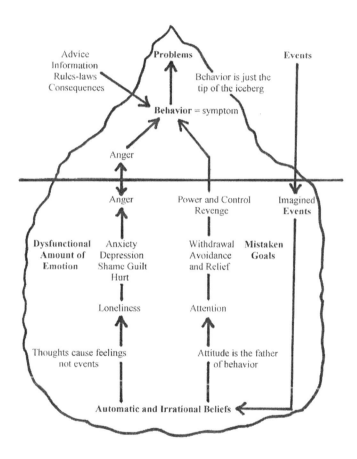

That is why an iceberg is a perfect metaphor for what's occurring when peoples' behavior is creating problems for them and others. Behavior is just the tip of the iceberg. Most people know that the bulk of an iceberg is below the surface and can't be seen, and that the unseen part is the dangerous part. So it is with behavior and it's underlying causes. Behavior can be seen, as can the symptoms of any problems it creates. People are also typically aware of their own and others life events, or at least can become aware of them with a little investigation. However, the vast number of automatic irrational beliefs that people can have in response to their life events, and the feelings and mistaken goals those give rise to, often go unrecognized by the people themselves, their friends and families, and sometimes even those trained to help them resolve behavioral issues. Those beliefs, feelings and mistaken goals are the bulk of the problem, and the most dangerous part. And, they typically do not respond to superficial attempts to change behavior. They are sometimes even exacerbated by those same attempts.

Remember that thoughts cause feelings, not events. Peoples' behavior follows their emotions toward their life events. And, as my friend Jerry Rankin always said while he was our dean of students, attitude is the father of behavior. That is why it is so important to look at how people think, no matter what age they are.

A Computer Metaphor

Most people know more about how computers work these days than they do about how their own brains work. There are many similarities. That is completely understandable since computers were after all modeled after human brains.

Computers can store vast amounts of data and text on their hard drives. If you click on a bar to the right of a very long word document and drag it downward, text and data can fly across a computer's screen so fast that it cannot be read or recognized. However, it is still there. If you slow it down, or better yet, print it out and trap it on paper, it becomes easily discernible. They are even some advantages to working with or proofing and editing a document's contents when it is in the form of a hard copy. However, no matter how fast text and data can fly across a screen, there can only be a limited amount of data or text on the screen at any given time.

So it is with human brains. People can store vast amounts of helpful advice, information, experiences, morals and values in their brains, all of which could be very important and helpful in any decisions they make. People also have a large volume of automatic irrational beliefs about themselves, others and every aspect of life. All this "data" or "text" can fly across the proverbial "screens" in their heads at very high speeds. It can be very much like a message board with the speed cranked up so fast that the messages cannot be read. It's there, but just can't be read. They can only be thinking one thought at a time, but they can go from one thought to another extremely fast, and what is on their "screens" at times when crucial choices must be made is more important than anything else. Automatic irrational beliefs can pass through peoples' consciousness so fast that if someone were to ask them what they were thinking when they felt a certain way or did something that was not the best thing to do, they would probably say, "I don't know". However, if their thought processes can be slowed down in some way, those automatic irrational beliefs become more discernible. And, if they can be trapped on paper, it's much easier to proof and edit them.

In terms of this metaphor, the problem is that too often peoples' automatic irrational beliefs about others, life, themselves, and a host of other things, get on their "screens" instead of helpful advice and information, past experiences, or morals and values. This causes them to generate a dysfunctional amount of emotion and make poor behavioral choices.

When people behave in unhealthy, self-defeating ways, these automatic irrational beliefs are the "irrational logic" of what they do. What people do is often irrational in that it makes their lives worse instead of better, but it is more understandable, and even somewhat logical, once others learn how they think.

A Computer Metaphor

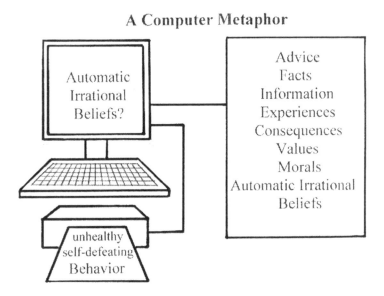

A sports analogy is also appropriate. If a team went into a game with only an offensive game plan, and no defensive one, they would be in trouble. Teams need both to have their best chance of winning. The advice and information teachers, books, magazines, radio and TV programs give people to prepare them for potentially troublesome life situations is like an offensive game plan. It's what teachers and experts in their fields suggest people think, feel, say and do in those situations.

However, these books, magazines, radio and TV programs usually neglect to give people a defensive game plan to deal with those automatic irrational beliefs that will often pop onto and dominate their "screen" at crucial times when decisions must be made. The best defense is NOT always a good offense.

This computer metaphor suggests questions and steps that could be taken to help people better manage what goes on inside their own heads in crucial situations where they and others often make mistakes.

1) What are some situations where people commonly make mistakes?

2) What might be on their "screen" when they make such mistakes?

    a) What might someone be thinking?

    b) What might they tell themselves

    c) What's might go through their heads?

3) Print out what they might think on paper. Trap it on paper

4) Teach them how to clear their screens of such thoughts.

5) What would it be helpful for them to have on their "screens" instead?

6) Rehearse and practice the process ahead of time

Brainstorming what people might be thinking or telling themselves when they make common mistakes to try to prevent future ones is analogous to what coaches do before they play an opposing team. It's "scouting" the opposition. Teaching people how to combat their automatic irrational beliefs and clear their "screen" is like developing a defensive game plan once the opposition's offense has been "scouted".

Most people have probably had their parents ask them "What were you thinking when you did something so stupid?" when they were young. That is the key question. Unfortunately, most parents just conclude, "The problem is you weren't thinking". People are always thinking, no matter how old they are, and it is what they are thinking that holds the key to any emotion they generate and any unhealthy or unacceptable behavior they engage in.

IRRATIONAL THINKING

A simple definition of irrational is that something people think, feel, say or do makes their life worse instead of better. Thinking is irrational if it causes people to generate a greater frequency, intensity or duration of feelings like anger, anxiety, depression, shame, guilt or loneliness than necessary or helpful, and then to behave in ways that make their lives worse instead of better.

Long ago, Dr. Albert Ellis postulated that there were four basic types of irrational thinking that cause people to feel worse than they need to, for longer than necessary, and to do irrational things that make their lives worse instead of better. He called them:

1) Demandiness
2) Awfulizing
3) Can't Stand It-it is
4) Label and Damning

He also postulated a "Wheel of Misfortune". Picture this wheel spinning like the TV version, only back and forth from one type of irrational thought to another, and at imperceptible speed. People might only verbalize one of the four types of thoughts, but the others will be there. Even if they do not verbalize any, if they experience feelings like anger, anxiety, depression, shame, guilt and loneliness, they will be generating these four types of automatic irrational beliefs.

DEMANDINESS

There are three basic ways to look at something. People can take the position that they don't care about whether they have or get something, or what happens. They can want, prefer or desire something, or want, prefer and desire things to be or turn out a certain way. Or, they can think they need something, it's a necessity, and demand it, or think things need to, have to, or must turn our a certain way.

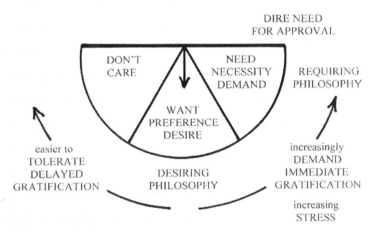

84

Rule #1: *You have the right to want whatever you want*

Others may not like or agree with what someone wants, but that person has a right to want it. Parents, for example, often don't like or agree with what their sons and daughters want. They sometimes even say, "You shouldn't want that", which often simply makes what the young person wanted a "forbidden fruit" and causes them to want it even more.

The problem, according to Dr. Ellis, is that humans have an apparently innate tendency to:

1) Think they need things they simply want
2) Treat their simple preferences as necessities
3) Demand what they simply desire

People need air, water and food, and possibly a few other things. They will die in minutes, days or weeks if they do not get them. Many people think they need love. They often cite Maslow's Hierarchy of Needs as proof. However, love is not the same as air, water and food. They will not die if they do not get all the love they would like, even if they think they need it. Otherwise, there would be a lot more dead people than there already are. There has never been a death certificate that listed the cause of death as "lack of love". There have however, been plenty of death certificates that listed the cause of death as "hypoxia" (lack of oxygen), "dehydration" or "malnutrition". When people think they need something they simply want, it's called a perceived need, as opposed to a biological need like air, water and food. Perceiving a simple want, preference or desire as a need or necessity, and then demanding it, is a simple but important underlying cause of so much that goes wrong in peoples' lives.

Rule #2: *The greater the difference between your expectations and reality, the more emotion you will generate, perhaps needlessly*

By thinking they need something that they simply want, by treating something they simply prefer as a necessity, and by demanding something they simply desire, people set the stage for generating more emotion than is necessary or helpful if and when they do not get what they want, prefer or desire. For example, if teachers truly do not care if their students talk while they are teaching, and their students do, they will not generate any emotion. Blessed are those who expect nothing for they shall not be disappointed. However, if teachers want their students to be quiet, and they're not, the teachers will be frustrated, irritated or annoyed. If those same teachers believe their students need to be, have to be, or must be quiet and they are not, those same teachers will generate anger. When students talk it is just an event. How much feeling or emotion teachers generate will depend on how they choose to look at the event of students talking, not on whether the students talk or not, or how much they do. This is the simple underlying mechanism by which people make themselves feel worse than necessary or helpful.

This is why anger and frustration are not simply stronger and weaker versions of the same emotion. They are qualitatively different. Frustration comes from wanting, preferring or desiring something and not getting it. Anger comes from people thinking need something, it is a necessity, and demanding it, and then not getting it. There can be varying degrees of intensity for both frustration and anger. People can be sort of frustrated, really frustrated, or somewhere in between. How frustrated they end up would depend on how much they wanted, preferred or desired something in the first place. However, once they cross that cognitive line, and start to demand it, they become angry.

People can make demands of others, themselves and life. Who or what they make demands of will determine the feeling they end up with.

If people make demands of others and those demands are not met, they will generate anger. Their basic demand is that everyone be the way they want them to be, and do what they want them to do. Road Rage is a perfect example. Hundreds or even thousands of people sitting in traffic want, prefer and desire to get where they want to go as fast as possible. They would all like the people in front of them to go faster. People do not like being impeded from getting where they want to go. However, people who generate road rage in themselves not only want, prefer and desire others get out of their way, but demand that everyone get out of their way immediately. People do not want others to cut them off. They don't like when others do. However, people who generate road rage have the attitude "How dare they do that to ME!" They demand that everyone else do exactly what they want right now, and not do anything they don't approve of? How old do people sound if they think that way? It sounds like they are two, three or four year olds. That is why Dr. Ellis called anger a "temper tantrum".

When people make demands of others, they often use the verbs "should" and "shouldn't" in constructing their thoughts and comments. Using "should" or "shouldn't" does not automatically mean people are being demanding. They could just be expressing a simple want, preference or desire. But when they mean others "have to" or "must" do what they want, it is jokingly called "shoulding" on others. People can also "should" on themselves. It is not helpful for people to "should" on themselves or "should" on others.

If people make demands of themselves before some upcoming event, they can experience anxiety. Their basic demand of themselves is that they always have to be perfect and do everything perfectly. For example, "I have to do well on this test. I can't make any mistakes. I have to get the best grade in the class".

The formula for anxiety is:

$$Catastrophizing + Awfulizing = Anxiety$$

Catastrophizing is simply imagining something bad happening. People are more likely to catastrophize when they go from simply wanting to do something to thinking they have to, or must do it a certain way, or perfectly. They are more likely to catastrophize if they not only want things to be or turn out a certain way, but start to think things need to, have to or must, and demand that they do. For example, a student who thinks they have to and must get a perfect score on a test is more likely to catastrophize than one who simply want to pass it anyway they can. People are also more likely to "awfulize" about something going wrong if they not only want, prefer and desire that it not happen, but think it can't and must not.

Much of what people call stress is typically just anxiety. If people listen to the way they and others talk when they feel stressed out, they would probably notice that they and others begin many of their comments with "I have to…" or "I can't…". Wanting to do things is a good thing. When people go from simply wanting to do something to thinking they have to or must, it becomes too much of a good thing. The attitudes that make people excel often morph into something that starts to destroy them.

I have been a Cub fan my entire life. People always say the Cubs have the greatest fans in the world. I have always said that that is part of the problem. When the stands are full every day, and fans are as supportive as they are of the Cubs, players not only want to win for them (and themselves), but also understandably might start to think they have to or must win. Add in the fact that the Cubs have not won a world series for over a century, something everyone talks about all the time, and it starts to become a big HAVE TO. This only serves to put undue stress on the team. I believe that explains their performance in last year's playoffs. They won over 100 games during the season, and lost three straight to the Dodgers. There are so many times in every kind of sport where an underdog upsets a much better team. This is probably the reason why. Underdogs play loose, like they have nothing to lose and everything to gain.

You see individuals put this same kind of stress on themselves too. Kerry Wood and Mark Pryor did it. They became good and rose to the top of their profession not only because they had talent, but probably because they wanted to excel so badly. After their stellar performances as rookies, fan expectations were very high. I truly believe Wood and Pryor started to demand a lot of themselves. They both started to have a lot of HAVE TO's in their heads. It's why I sadly predicted to my students who were die-hard Cub fans that they would both probably end up injured from unrelenting stress. Carlos Zombrano has done the same thing in his head ever since he got his big contract. Talent and wanting to be the Cub's number one starter took him to the top, but once he got there, and got the big money, too many of those wants morphed into HAVE TOs.

If people make demands of themselves after an event, they can generate shame and guilt. They would basically be "shoulding" on themselves. They would be telling themselves that they should have, had to or must have done something different, more or better than what they did. They think or say things like "I should have known better", "I should have seen this coming", "I shouldn't have let this happen", or "I should have been there".

Loneliness can also come from people making demands of themselves. For example, they might think they should, have to, or must have more friends than they do, or have a boyfriend or girlfriend, and don't. Or, they might think they should be married like all their friends, and they are not. Feeling lonely is not caused by being alone. That is just an event. It is what people think about being alone that either causes loneliness, or does not.

If people make demands of life, they can feel depressed or bored. They are basically saying that their life should not, cannot or must not be the way it is. It should, has to, or must be easier, more pleasant, more fun and other things than it is. And it is not. For example, "This can't be happening to us", "It can't be", "It's not fair", "Someone should do something about this", or "Teachers should make school more fun and interesting" and "School shouldn't be so hard". Dr. Ellis called depression brought on by such irrational demands a "quiet temper tantrum". Boredom is the product of a quiet temper tantrum as well. Of course, if people have ever been teachers, they know it is not always quiet.

Demanding that everything in their life go exactly as they want, would like or plan can cause people to needlessly generate anxiety. If people quietly demand that they not get sick, they can generate needless anxiety about their health. If they implicitly demand that they never have to die like everyone else, they can generate anxiety about death and dying.

I actually got to do a demonstration of REBT therapy with Dr. Ellis a while back. At the time, I periodically struggled with anxiety about death and dying, so I figured I'd give him a crack at helping me with it. He was in his late eighties at the time, and I suspect the idea of his own death had crossed his mind. We talked for only a short while and I elaborated on my anxiety. I still remember what he asked me. "Why should you get to live forever when no one else does? Why must life treat you any better or more fairly than it does anyone else including me?" (I cleaned this up. Dr. Ellis liked to use colorful language for emphasis) He was right on target. There was nothing wrong with me wanting, preferring and desiring to live as long as I could. I still do. It's why I wear my seat belt, exercise daily and eat right among other things. However, I had gone too far. I was demanding that nothing happen to me, ever. That created a huge gap between my expectations of life and the reality that anyone can die unexpectedly sooner than they would like. That caused the anxiety.

Rule #3: *Starting to think you need something you simply want, to treat a simple preference as a necessity, and to demand what you simply desire, will make otherwise smart people do stupid things.*

The reason is simple. If people were suffocating, what would they be willing to do to get air? Anything! If people not only want others to love them, but start to think they need for them to, and that they could not live without other peoples' love, what would they be willing to do to get the love they think they so desperately need? The answer's the same. Anything. And that is what makes otherwise smart people do stupid things.

Rule #4: *Behavior intended to satisfy a perceived need will win out over behavior intended to satisfy a rational preference*

Wanting to quit smoking would be a rational preference. However, if people think they need cigarettes and cannot go a whole day without them, their chances of quitting are not very good. If they want to smoke, but also want to quit, it could go either way.

Given all the things that could go wrong, if a girl wants to wait until she is married to have sex, that would be a completely rational preference. However, if she not only wants her boyfriend to love her, but also thinks she needs his love and could not live without him, and he wants sex, she is more likely to give in. If she simply wants or would like for him to love her, but wants to wait, it could go either way.

Many of today's problems are caused by people wanting immediate gratification of every want, preference or desire they have. When people start to think they need something they simply want, to treat a preference as a necessity, and to demand what they simply desire, they will be less likely to tolerate delayed gratification. Businesses who sell products that make peoples' lives more comfortable, convenient and pleasurable have used clever advertisements to encourage people to think they need things instead of simply want them, that such things are necessities to their lives rather than simple preferences, and to demand more comfort, convenience and pleasure than they already have. Then businesses develop promotions like "no interest, no payments for 12 months" to make it easier for people to have those things they now think they need, and have to, or must have, even if they cannot afford them. People do not want or like to go deep into debt, but they start to think they need things they simply wanted, and it makes them do stupid things. It is the reason why personal debt is such a common and major problem in so many households and lives. It is also the reason we are a "pill" society. People not only want, but demand that they feel better quickly and easily, without them having to change the way they live to help themselves.

People develop a tolerance for comfort, convenience and pleasure, as well as wealth, like they do for alcohol and drugs and so many other things. It starts to take more for them to experience the same satisfaction they once did with less. This sets the stage for discontentment with life, regardless of how pleasant, convenient or comfortable peoples' reality might appear to the eyes of others. However, it starts when people go from simply wanting, preferring and desiring more comfort, convenience and pleasure to thinking they need it, it is a necessity, and start to demand it.

If you ask teachers why many students are not doing well, many will say it is because too many students simply do not want to do the work assigned, and want everything to be easy and fun. It is human nature to want life to be more pleasant, convenient and comfortable than it already is. As noted above, it is also human nature to develop tolerances for everything including pleasantness, convenience and comfort. Our entire society not only wants life to be ever more pleasant, convenient and comfortable, but often demands that it be. People have been encouraged to demand it be by industries who develop and profit from selling an ever-growing list of products that make life just that. Kids often not only mimic adult attitudes and attributes but also magnify them, sometimes to a point of being absurd. It is no wonder that so many of today's students don't want to work.

In summary, so many of the problems facing individuals,

families, schools and our society as a whole can be explained by the simple human tendencies identified by Dr. Ellis decades ago. Those tendencies are for people to think they need things they simply want, to treat their simple preferences as necessities, and to demand what they simply desire. As people go from simply wanting, preferring and desiring something to thinking they need it, it is a necessity, and demanding it, they set the stage cognitively to experience a dysfunctional amount of emotion if they do not get what they want, prefer or desire. This is turn makes them more likely to have "mistaken" goals and gives more purpose to any unhealthy, self-defeating behavior they might engage in. As people go from a desiring to a requiring philosophy, they also tend to be more prone to expect and demand immediate gratification of every want, preference or desire, and this sets the stage for discontentment and unhappiness. They are also more likely to experience unnecessary stress. People create unnecessary stress for themselves when they go from simply wanting to do something to thinking they HAVE TO.

Demands can often be disguised as questions. For example, if people say something like, "How dare they talk to me like that?" or "How could someone act like that?", they are making a demand of others. The demands are that others should not, cannot, and must not talk to them the way they do, or act the way they do. Others should, have to and must talk to them the way they want others to, and act the way they think is appropriate. If people say things like "How could I have missed that?" or "How could I have been so stupid?", they are making demands of themselves. The demands are that they should not, cannot and must not make mistakes. They should, have to and must be perfect and do everything perfectly all the time.

People have a right to want whatever they want, but it is important that they avoid telling themselves that they need something they simply want. It is important that people avoid or stop treating their simple preferences as necessities. Last, it is important people avoid, or stop demanding what they simply desire. Adults know that it is not healthy for a child to be demanding, and that giving in to his or her demands sets the stage for a variety of emotional and behavioral problems later. That is an important thing to remember. It works that way when people become adults too.

AWFULIZING

There are a lot of things in life that are unpleasant, inconvenient or uncomfortable. The mistake people make is to start to perceive such things as awful. When I was a child, my grandfather would always tell me I was "making a mountain out of a molehill". That is what people basically do when they "awfulize".

Paradoxically, the easier life gets, the easier it becomes for people to do that. It is easy, for example, for students to think it is awful and terrible that someone calls them a name or spreads a rumor about them at school when nothing much else is happening in their lives. They can choose to attach an undue amount of importance and awfulness to that event. However, if they suddenly received a call at school saying a parent had a heart attack and may not make it, the name-calling would instantly be displaced to its proper place of being something that was simply, and just slightly unpleasant.

Not everyone in the USA has as pleasant, convenient or comfortable a life as everyone else. However, compared to many other places in the world, most people in the USA do live a pleasant, convenient and comfortable life, and one that is much more pleasant, convenient and comfortable than what most people in the course of human history ever have. Awfulizing has become rather pervasive because of this. Having news coverage 24 hours a day, 7 days a week has caused networks and cable channels to compete more than ever for viewers by sensationalizing stories. Sensationalizing on the part of news outlets is probably translating into awfulizing in the general public.

As I noted earlier, I make regular trips from one end of the country to the other and listen to talk radio to stay awake. I spent much of my life trying to get my students, friends and family members to disturb themselves less, and to not disturb themselves needlessly. To do that, I needed to know the mechanisms by which people do disturb themselves. That's why I recognize that many nationally syndicated talk radio hosts skillfully encourage their listeners to inflame themselves needlessly on a daily basis using those same mechanisms. They do it by presenting their listeners with probable, but unlikely political and economic scenarios (catastrophizing) and talking about how awful things are and will be (awfulizing) if such things happen. I use the formula for anxiety (catastrophizing + awfulizing = anxiety) to show people how to disturb themselves less. They use the formula for anxiety to bring their listeners to the point of plugging into their "fight or flight" mechanisms and then offer political and ideological opponents as scapegoats for the anger that goes with that intense anxiety.

People often say, "It's just a figure of speech" when they are challenged about "awfulizing". However, the words people use to describe their experience are important. The top portion of peoples' brains is connected to the outside world by way of their eyes and ears. The lower portion that generates feelings and controls body functions is not. It is blind and deaf. It relies on the top portion to let it know whether things are going well or badly, whether it is safe or there are threats, and how big any threats are. It takes the word of the top portion. The top portion uses words to interpret and evaluate its experience. The words people use to describe their experience are important, and do make a qualitative and quantitative difference in the frequency, intensity and duration of any emotion they generate.

"I Can't Stand It"-itis

Rule #5: *You have a right to like or dislike whatever you want to*

People have a right to like or dislike whatever they want to. The mistake people make is when they start to tell themselves they cannot stand something they simply do not like. If people truly and literally could not stand something, they would die or go crazy. If all the people who said they could not stand something were telling the truth, there would be dead bodies or insane people everywhere. The truth is that people simply do not like a lot of things that happen to them, and that's their right. They can stand it. They just do not like it. However, by telling themselves they cannot stand something they simply do not like, they inflame themselves needlessly. That is why Dr. Ellis called this type of irrational thinking "I can't stand it-ITIS".

I can't stand it-ITIS is a big part of an emotional state that many of today's students generate in themselves that makes it much harder for them to do work they are asked to do. It is called Low Frustration Tolerance (LFT). Here is what it sounds like:

I can't stand doing things that are boring
I can't stand doing the same thing all the time
I can't stand doing problems EVERY day
I can't stand doing things I don't see the point to
I can't stand getting homework every night
I can't stand getting up so early to come to school

Remember, if you have one type of thought, Dr. Ellis said you would have the others. For example,

It's really awful that we have so much work
It's really awful that we have to do such boring things
It's really awful that we have to come to school every day
We shouldn't have to do things we don't like
We shouldn't have to do so much work every day
We should be able to do whatever we want
Teachers should make school more fun
Teachers should let us do whatever we want

Dr. Ellis called the type of thinking "Whining". Most teachers have heard such comments many times and rightfully recognize it as "whining" too. Many adults in modern day America are guilty of similar thinking. Once again, as life becomes more pleasant, convenient and comfortable, and people develop a tolerance for it, they will be become increasingly intolerant of unpleasantness, inconvenience and discomfort. They are more likely to think they cannot stand things they simply do not like.

LABEL AND DAMNING

When people Label and Damn others or themselves, it is like calling an apple "bad" simply because it has a bruise on it, even though the vast majority of the apple is still perfectly edible. It is blatant overgeneralization. Racism is an example. Name-calling and put-downs are too. People are often told to condemn the deed and not the doer. Label and damning is exactly the opposite. It is condemning the doer instead of the deed.

However, just because people do things that others do not like does not make them jerks, stupid, lazy or anything else. Not doing what others want does not make them that either. Smart people can do stupid things. Nice people can do bad things. There are hundreds or even thousands of attributes, characteristics and behaviors that define who people are. No one of those says a lot about them. All people do by label and damning others is to inflame themselves needlessly. All people do by label and damning themselves is to needlessly generate the shame that can block change for the better.

Label and damning is encouraged daily in large listening audiences by nationally syndicated talk radio show hosts.

These hosts regularly create "straw men" by misrepresenting the positions of political and ideological opponents and never letting their opponents speak for themselves or present opposing points of view and the rationale for those views. They blatantly over generalize about the positions of those opponents, lumping anyone who disagrees with them into one big category. Most of them profess to represent a conservative point of view, but it is often a corporate-friendly point of view more than anything else, and the majority of radio stations across the country are now owned by a relatively few large corporations. These hosts have succeeded in making Democrat and Liberal dirty words for their listeners. The other side sometimes does the same, but there are fewer of them to do it. No matter who does it, it is unhealthy for people and the country.

I was always aware and concerned about how so many young people labeled and damned themselves, and how it impaired their ability to learn and be educated. Young people who struggle early on in school might understandably often conclude that it means they are stupid. They often get help and encouragement for concluding that from other students, their teachers and parents. Consider the impact on their behavior in school of establishing that perspective of themselves early in life. By the way, people do not feel stupid. Stupid is not a feeling. It is a perception. They think they are stupid. It is the meaning they attach to the past events of their lives, like failing tests or not understanding or getting something when everyone else did. They feel shame and guilt about past performances, and can generate intense anxiety about impending ones. That anxiety would cause them to dread challenges and opportunities rather than welcome them, and make them do anything to avoid the possibility of failing and feeling their old familiar way.

Anxiety is a figment of imagination. First people "catastrophize" or imagine something bad happening and then they tell themselves that it would be awful if it did. It is understandable for people to imagine something bad happening if they believe that they did not live up to their own or others expectations in the past and perceived many past performances as turning out awful. It is also understandable that they might conclude it means they are stupid. That is what people often do. However, that is not the only thing it could mean. If people have had a history of failing tests, or even classes, all it means for sure is that they did not know everything that someone else wanted them to know, as well as that person wanted them to know it, when they wanted them to. There could be a multitude of reasons why they did not, and it does not have to mean they are stupid. For example, boys sometimes develop slower intellectually than girls. Some kids could go home every night to alcoholic parents and struggle to let go of what happened the night before when they come to school the next day. If their work and grades are below what they and others would like, that does not have to mean they are stupid.

If young people do not do exactly what teachers, parents or other adults want them to, when those people want them to, it does not make them "bad" either. It does not make them a "problem", "disobedient", "disrespectful" or anything else. It is understandable for teachers, parents and others to label and damn children who do not do what they ask them to, or who do things they don't like. It is human nature. However, behavior often has complex causes, and being quick to label and damn students who do not do what teachers want, when they want, is not helpful. This is especially true since the perceptions teachers develop are not simply a product of what students do. What students do is just an event, no matter how outrageous teachers might think it is. What teachers expect in the first place makes a big difference in how they perceive what students do. Some teachers can be so demanding of obedience and respect that any transgression, no matter how insignificant it might appear to be to others, could be seen as something "awful" and terrible, and something that they "can't stand".

Alex Molnar and Barbara Lindquist wrote an excellent book entitled "Changing Problem Behavior in Schools". They talk about "frozen perceptions" that teachers develop about misbehaving students, many of which are nothing more than examples of label and damning. These "frozen perceptions" get passed along from teacher to teacher, from grade to grade, through official school records, and by word of mouth. They lock both teachers and students into destructive cognitive, emotional and behavioral patterns that only make matters worse and prevent teachers from finding solutions to what they consider behavior problems. Problems with students are often simply misbehaviors that get mismanaged. Their suggestion: try finding a new way to look at what students do that is not so negative and unflattering, and perhaps positive in some way, and start behaving toward students from that new perspective and see what happens.

IDENTIFYING IRRATIONAL BELIEFS

Sometimes people verbalize their automatic irrational beliefs. For example, people say things like, "How dare they do that?" (demand), "They can't tell me what to do!" (demand), "They should mind their own business" (demand), "It's really awful when they do that" (awfulizing), "I can't stand when people say things like that" (can't stand it-itis) or "He's an idiot" (label and damning). However, automatic irrational beliefs often go unspoken.

Thoughts always cause feelings, and attitude is always the father of behavior. Peoples' emotions and behavior often won't change until their thoughts, attitudes or beliefs do. Most irrational beliefs are the product of much practice and rehearsal, and therefore automatic. People can often be relatively unaware of such beliefs because of that. If people are not in touch with what their automatic irrational beliefs are, it is harder for them to know what they need to change. It is important for people to get in touch with their automatic irrational beliefs, especially if those beliefs are causing them to generate a dysfunctional amount of emotion and behave in unhealthy, self-defeating ways that make their lives worse.

As noted earlier, if people have one of the four types of irrational thoughts, they will have the other three too. Their "Wheel of Misfortune" will be spinning and they will be generating one type of irrational thought after another. If people verbalize one type of irrational belief, it can be a clue as to what their other irrational beliefs might be. Even if no automatic irrational beliefs are verbalized, the evidence that those thoughts are there will be the dysfunctional amount of emotion that they generate, and the irrational way they behave.

There are some simple but important questions that an REBT therapist might ask clients to help identify their automatic irrational beliefs. People can ask themselves or others these same questions. For example:

1) What would you (I) have to be thinking or telling yourself (myself) to make yourself (myself) feel that way?

2) If your (my) behavior could talk, what would it say?

3) What might the way you (I) act say about how you (I) look at or see things?

4) What might you (I) be trying to tell others by acting the way you (I) do?

What does not come out in words often comes out in behavior.

According to Terry London, identifying automatic irrational

beliefs has two names. One is "Thought catching", the other is "Making public speech out of private talk". The first reflects the fact that such thoughts fly through someone's consciousness at high speed because of prior practice and rehearsal. It is like a message board whose speed has been cranked up so fast that people cannot read the messages. They are there. They just can't read them because the messages are flying by too fast. People can be unable to verbalize what their automatic irrational beliefs are for the same reason. They occur at high speed and one after another. The second term reflects the fact that the majority of irrational thought goes unspoken. Many unhealthy, self-defeating behaviors occur because people keep secrets, and their automatic irrational beliefs go unchallenged.

To brainstorm what my own or others' demands might be, I methodically work through a chart like the one below, combining pronouns with common verb phrases that people use when being demanding. The pronoun that gets used to brainstorm demands will largely depend on which feeling people are generating. Remember, when people are angry, they are making demands of others. When people feel shame and guilt, they are making demands of themselves. If they are depressed or bored they are making demands of life. Anxiety can come from making demands of themselves or life

	He, She They	I	This, It
How dare…	___		
How could…	___	___	___
need to…	___	___	___
have (has) to…	___	___	___
can't…	___	___	___
should…	___	___	___
shouldn't…	___	___	___

Here is an example that I would do with my classes as part of the sex education unit. A young girl and guy are dating. She would prefer to wait until she is married to have sex, but he wants to have sex now. They get into regular arguments about what to do and ruin much of their time together because of it.

The real events for her would be that he gets mad at her and they fight and argue. However, there are probably a host of events that she might imagine because they fight. For example, she might imagine that he will break up with her, he will go out with someone else, and he will do something with someone else instead of her. She might also imagine that he will spread nasty rumors about her, that others will believe them, and that she will never have a boyfriend again and end up alone. Brainstorming all the possible imagined events is important because it will make brainstorming irrational beliefs easier, especially the "awfulizing" and "I can't stand it-itis" variety.

All the imagined events above are possibilities. However, if she said, "So what, who cares?" she probably would not generate anxiety (or guilt) and give in. So what would she have to tell herself to generate intense anxiety and end up doing what he wants instead of what she wants?

Anxiety is a figment of imagination. It's an emotional reaction to things that haven't happened yet. To generate anxiety, she would have to make demands of herself or life before some event actually ever happened. She would have to be telling herself that she needed something instead of simply wanted it; that she should, had to, needed to, or must do something; and that her life had to, or must be a certain way. She would have to tell herself that she should not, could not, and must not do something else; and that she couldn't live without something, or let something happen.

When I did this activity with my classes, I would simply say a phrase out loud, write it on the board, and sometimes keep repeating it, letting my students finish it. I would write the way they completed the phrase after lines springing from it. For example, "I need...", or "I can't...". That's called brainstorming. It was as if I started them down some pathway in their brain, and they told me where it ended up. The fact that they were able to complete such phrases relatively easily suggested to me that they had either had such thoughts themselves, or had heard others make such comments. The quicker and easier it was for them to complete the phrases I gave them, the more likely it was that they had thought or heard the resulting thought many times before. It was also more likely it was one of the automatic irrational beliefs that they might have in a relationship.

The following are some possible automatic irrational beliefs this girl might have:

I need him

I need to be with him

I need his love

I need a boyfriend

I can't let him break up with me

I can't let him go out with someone else

I can't let him do it with someone else instead of me

I I can't be alone

I can't be without a boyfriend

I can't keep saying "No" to him

I can't risk losing him

I have to do what he wants

I have to make/keep him happy

I have to make him want to stay with me

I should have done it by now (guilt)

I should just do it and get it over with

I shouldn't have made him so mad (guilt)

I shouldn't have said "No" to him   (guilt)

Brainstorming "awfulizing" and "I can't stand it-itis" beliefs is relatively simple in a case of anxiety, especially if all the possible imagined events have been identified. It simply involves adding the real (past, present) and imagined (future) events to the phrases listed below.

It's really awful that/when + real event

It'd be awful if + imagined event

I can't stand when + real event

I couldn't stand it if + imagined event

I'd just die if + imagined event

For example:

It's really awful when he gets mad at me

It'd be awful if he broke up with me

It'd be awful if he went out with someone else

It'd be awful if he did it with them instead of me

I can't stand when he gets mad at me

I couldn't stand losing him

I couldn't stand seeing him with someone else

I'd just die if he did it with someone else

Brainstorming possible "label and damning" beliefs is done in a similar fashion. A common way people start such thoughts is with a phrase like "I'd be stupid to…"

I'd be stupid to keep saying "No" to him

I'd be stupid to let him break up with me

I'd be stupid to let him go out with someone else

I'd be stupid to let him spread rumors about me

An additional belief a young girl might unfortunately have is:

There must be something wrong with me because I haven't done it yet

Now consider this. There is a regular on-going debate over what to do about teen pregnancies and STDs in young people. There are those who believe an abstinence-only approach is best, and others who believe a comprehensive sex education approach is better. Suppose this girl took part in an abstinence-only based curriculum, a comprehensive sex education program, or even both, and even did very well on quizzes and tests. If she thought this way, would anything she learned in either type of program probably keep her from giving in and perhaps making the same mistake so many young girls have made? Probably not.

Here is another example. A male student regularly gets into fights whenever someone calls him a name. He has been punished repeatedly and the consequences have escalated, but his behavior does not seem to respond to anything that the school does to him. If his behavior could talk, what might it say? What might the way he acts say about how he looks at or see things? What would he have to be thinking or telling himself to make him so angry and cause him to keep getting into trouble no matter how much he gets punished for it? What might he even be trying to tell others by acting the way he does?

The fighting is most likely driven by anger. People get angry because they make demands of others. They basically say that others should not, cannot, and must not do what they do. Others should, have to, or must do what they want, and be the way they want them to be. Sometimes those demands will come in the form of a question starting with "How dare they…?" Or "How could they…?".

Using the same procedure as before, here are some possible automatic irrational beliefs this young man might have that would explain his anger and recurrent misbehavior:

How dare they say that to me?

They can't say things like they about me

They can't call me that

They can't get away with that

They shouldn't call people names

I can't let them get away with that

I can't let them talk to me like that

I can't let them think they can treat me like that

I have to teach them a lesson

I have to make them stop calling me names

I have to make them pay for that

It's really awful when people call me names

I can't stand being called names

They're idiots for calling me names like that

Thoughts like the above that produce anger are called "hot" thoughts. If school authorities wonder why no amount of consequences have worked, it's because he tells himself that he HAS TO get even, and CAN'T let them get away with it, no matter what.

Sometimes consequences can reduce or extinguish a behavior. However, too often they do not, and we see repeat offenses. Peoples' behavior follows their emotion toward their life events. Thoughts always cause feelings, not events. Attitude is always the father of behavior. Would consequences really do anything to address or change the underlying thoughts or beliefs this student has that cause his anger, or the attitudes that father his behavior? Too often consequences have no real effect on underlying attitudes and beliefs, and might even exacerbate them instead. For example, if one of the attitudes that father misbehavior is that a student thinks "They can't do that to me", imposing consequences would not cause them to stop thinking that way, and might even cause them to be more likely to.

Brainstorming possible automatic irrational beliefs is analogous in some ways to running a blood test. When people acknowledge that a particular belief sounds familiar, it's like some value being high or low on a blood test. It tells people exactly what's wrong with them, and what they need to fix.

CORRECTING IRRATIONAL THINKING

Learning to recognize irrational thinking in oneself and others is an important life skill to have. Learning to correct it is as important, if not more.

Sometimes Demands come in the form of a question. They start with phrases like "How dare they…?" or "How could they…?" For example:

How dare they say that about me?

How could they act like that?

Basically, someone is saying that others cannot, should not, or must not say what they are, or act the way they are. The facts are that people can say and do whatever they want, even if others do not like it. And it does not take a lot of energy, effort or intelligence to do so. That is why the REBT answer to all such questions is always "EASILY!

A person can also make similar demands of him or herself. If the demand is in a question form and directed at oneself, the answer would be the same. For example:

How could I have been so stupid?

EASILY! It's because I am Fallible Human Being like everyone else.

The first time people are told that answer, they more often than not smile and laugh a little. That's good! It's better than getting angry needlessly. Perhaps it is because they realize the silliness of demanding that everyone else be the way they want and do what they want, and suggesting that others cannot be any other way, or do anything else.

Here is the big picture when it comes to correcting irrational thinking. In essence, every thought people have is basically a theory or hypothesis about how life around them is, or should be. The greater the difference between peoples' theories and hypotheses about how things are or should be, and they really are, the more emotion people will generate needlessly. The closer peoples' theories are to reality, the less emotion they'll generate, and the more functional the amount they generate will be. It is that simple.

The degree of difference between peoples' theories and hypotheses and reality can also be seen as a measure of mental health. The greater the difference between their theories and hypotheses and reality, the less mental health people will enjoy. If the difference becomes too great and chronic, people head into the realm of mental illness. On the other hand, the closer peoples' theories and hypotheses come to matching reality, the more mentally healthy they will be.

The important question is, does the evidence of peoples' life support their theories or hypotheses, or does it perhaps refute them and suggest alternative ones instead. Here is an example

I saw many times in my school. A student walks out of the dean's office in a high school with a detention slip in his hand saying and thinking, "They can't give me a detention for that. It's not fair!" Does the evidence support his theories and hypotheses? The detention slip in his hand actually refutes his first one. The difference between his theory or hypothesis about how life should be and reality is as big as it can be. That is why he's angry and will stay angry as long as he continues to demand that school officials must not give him a detention. When someone says, "It's not fair", there is also an implicit demand that life should, has to, and must always be fair according to his or her definition of fairness. Good luck on that one.

One of the simplest ways for people to question, challenge or dispute irrational thinking in themselves and others is to ask, "Is that a fact or just an opinion?" When people disturb themselves needlessly, it is because they are thinking in terms of opinions rather than facts. The way for people to start generating a more functional amount of emotion, and to better tolerate things they do not like but cannot control, is to start thinking more in terms of facts rather than opinions. Here are some examples:

Opinion: They can't tell me what to do
Fact: People can say and do whatever they want
Opinion: They have to show me respect
Fact: They don't have to do anything

Opinion: It's really awful that they did that
Fact: It's not the end of the world
Opinion: I can't stand when people do that
Fact: I'll survive no matter what they do
Opinion: He's an idiot for doing that
Fact: I don't like when people do that

In the student example above, "They can't give me a detention for that" is just his opinion. So is "It's not fair"? Suppose he were to instead say, "Well, I don't like it, but they can do whatever they want". "I don't like it" might be an opinion, but when he verbalizes it under these circumstances, it is a fact. He really does not like it. "They can do whatever they want" is also a fact. If he were to think or say this instead of "They can't give me a detention for that", he would not be happy about getting one, but it would allow him to generate a more functional amount of emotion and tolerate what he does not like better. He would be less likely to do something else that would make his life even worse.

Schools teach the scientific method in science classes all over the country, but rarely if ever teach students to apply it to their theories and hypotheses about everyday life. That is a simple but important thing schools could start doing. It would not require any new teachers, classes or money to start doing it. Teachers would benefit immensely if they also started applying the scientific method to their everyday theories and hypotheses about their job, students and their own lives.

Another way to correct irrational thinking is to dispute, question and challenge it by asking simple, but pointed questions. It is important to be simple but precise when disputing, questioning or challenging demands right from the very start. To really develop truly effective emotional management, the process of identifying and correcting automatic irrational beliefs needs to become automatic, like spell or grammar check on computers. It takes a good deal of rehearsal and practice for the process to become automatic, and it is important that people always rehearse or practice disputing the correct way from the very start. I have seen many times what happens if they do not. It erodes the effectiveness of disputing.

In the following examples, B = Belief, D = Dispute or question, and A = Answer to the dispute or question.

Look at the diagram below. There are always three basic ways to look at something. People can take the position that they don't care about something. They can want, prefer or desire it. Or, they can think they need it, it's a necessity, and demand it. Remember, people have a right to want, prefer or desire whatever they want. The mistake people make is to start to think they need something they simply want, to think they have to have something they simply would prefer, and to demand something they simply desire. With that in mind, here are the specific questions people can ask others and themselves.

Example 1

B: I need his love (demand of self, life)

D: Why do you need his love?

Do you need his love, or just want it?

Do you need his love like you need air, water and food?

You'd die if you didn't get air. Would you die if you didn't get his love?

When students or adults are first asked a question like, "Why do you need his love?" the first word out of their mouths is usually "Because...". Anything that follows the "Because..." is not the right answer. It often takes quite a while for people to realize what the correct answer is. Sometimes they simply have to be given the correct answer. The correct answers are:

A: I (you) don't need his love

COGNITIVE CHOICES

DIRE NEED
FOR APPROVAL

DON'T CARE

NEED
NECESSITY
DEMAND

REQUIRING
PHILOSOPHY

WANT
PREFERENCE
DESIRE

easier to
TOLERATE
DELAYED
GRATIFICATION

DESIRING
PHILOSOPHY

increasingly
DEMAND
IMMEDIATE
GRATIFICATION

increasing
STRESS

I (you) don't need his love, I (you) just want it

I (you) don't need his love like I (you) need air, water and food

I'm (you're) not going to die if I (you) don't get his love

Example 2

B: They have to show me respect (demand of others)

D: Why do they have to show you respect?

They have to, or you just want them to?

They have to, or you'd just like them to?

Why must they show you respect?

A: They don't have to show me (you) respect

They don't have to, I (you) just want them to

They don't have to, I'd (you'd) just like them to

They don't have to do anything

Example 3

B: They can't say that about me (demand of others)

D: Why can't they say that about you?

They can't, or you just don't want them to?

They can't, or you just don't like when they do?

A: They can say that about me (you)

They can, I (you) just don't want them to

They can, I (you) just don't like when they do

They can say whatever they want to

Example 4

B: I have to get an A on this test (demand of self)

D: Why do you have to get an A?

You have to, or just want to?

You have to, or would just like to?

Why must you get an A?

A: I (you) don't have to get an A

I (you) don't have to, I (you) just want to (and that's good!)

I (you) don't have to, I'd (you'd) just like to

I (you) don't have to do anything

Example 5

B: This can't be happening to me (demand of life)

D: Why can't this be happening to you?

It can't, or you just don't want it to?

It can't, or you just don't like that it is?

A: It can be happening to me (you)

It can be, I (you) just don't want it to be

It can be, I (you) just don't like that it is

The end products of such disputation are life lessons that people should learn early in life, but often do not, or forget. For example:

1) Other people do not have to do what we want

2) We do not have to do what others want

3) No one has to do anything.

People might have to live with some natural or manufactured consequences if they don't do something, but they don't HAVE TO do anything. My grandfather would always say, "You don't have to do anything except die and pay taxes". At least he was half right.

Parents want their children to learn lesson one, but are often fearful of their children learning lessons two and three. There is no real reason to be afraid of them learning the truth. For example, if children were to tell their parents, "I don't have to do what you want. I don't have to do anything", the simple and truthful response would be, "You're right. You don't have to do what I want. You don't have to do anything. And, I don't have to do what you want either. I don't have to do anything either." It is important children learn the principle of reciprocity. No one has to do anything, but if children want others to do things for them, perhaps even things others really do not want or like to do, then they might have to sometimes do things they might not want or like to do for others.

Conversely:

1) People can say and do whatever they want
2) They often will, regardless of how severe potential consequences might be

Finally, and perhaps most importantly:

1) Life isn't always fair, fun or easy,
2) It doesn't have to be, and often won't be.

Parents and teachers often hear demands from young people that start with "We should be able to…" or "We shouldn't have to…". For example:

We should be able to drink like everyone else can

We shouldn't have to wait until we're 21 to drink

In essence, they are saying that they should be able to do whatever they want, whenever they want, and should not have to do things they do not like, do not see the point to, or do not agree with. The tendency for many parents and teachers is to respond with "Well you can't…" and "Well, you do…", followed by an "…and, that's all there is to it". This typically only invites young people to have the mistaken goals of power and control, puff up their chest and courage, and do something stupid just to prove a point. Parents and their children get locked into unnecessary and futile power struggles. However, those responses are not true. They are not facts. The correct answers to the demand that they should be able to do whatever they want are:

You can.

You can do whatever you want to.

You can, you just might have to live with the consequences.

The correct answers to the second demand that they shouldn't have to do things they don't like or want to are:

You don't.

You don't have to do anything.

You don't, you just might have to live with the consequences if you don't.

Responding this way is called "taking the wind out of their sails". It takes away much of the motivation young people often have for doing things we do not want them to. Of course, adults also can do whatever they want to them, and adults do not have to let them, or make it easy for them to do things adults do not want them to do.

:

Affirming the Preference

When disputing the demands made by others, it helps to first affirm their preference before doing so. Remember, they have a right to want, prefer and desire whatever they want. The mistake they make is going from simply wanting, preferring and desiring something to thinking they need it, it is a necessity, and demanding it.

When affirming peoples' want, preference or desire before disputing their perceived need, or irrational necessity or demand, start what with phrases like:

I can understand why…

I agree that it would be nice if…

I know you want…

I realize that…

For example:

B:	They should mind their own business (demand of others)
ATP:	I agree that it would be nice if everyone minded his or her own business
	I can understand why you'd want them to, BUT,

D: Why do they have to mind their own business?
They have to, or you'd just like them to?
Why must they mind their own business?

DISPUTING AWFULIZING

Refer to the diagram on page 133. There are three basic ways people can look at something that happens that they do not like. One is that they don't care about it. The second is that they think it is unpleasant, inconvenient, or uncomfortable. Third, they can think it is awful. The mistake people make is to start to perceive things that are simply unpleasant, inconvenient, and uncomfortable to some degree as awful. Awful suggests that something is the worst possible thing that could happen and that life would no longer be worth living if it did. There are a lot of things in life that are unpleasant, inconvenient or uncomfortable. But are they really awful?

I was born in 1950. I grew up surrounded by adults who had grown up themselves during the Great Depression and who had been through World War II, and the United States was still embroiled in the Korean War, and the Cold War was hot and heavy. My grandparents had also lived through World War I. If I ever said something was "awful" or acted like it was, I didn't get a lot of sympathy. I remember very clearly being told many times, "Be quiet. You don't have an idea just how bad things can be. You've got a roof over your head and food on the table. It could be a lot worse."

We never had air conditioning back then. TV was black and white and there were only four channels and getting a clear picture was a real trick with the antennas. Everyone in the family didn't have their own car. We walked most places or rode the bus or subway. Houses were a lot smaller. There was no real fast food, no mega stores, no cell phones, no computers, and no credit cards. When I started teaching we typed carbon ditto masters on manual typewriters, and had to run copies off by hand. After 100 copies you had to make another master. By the time I retired, copiers did everything but make coffee. Remember that earlier in this book I noted a paradox that exists. The easier life gets, the more likely human beings are to perceive something that is simply unpleasant, inconvenient and uncomfortable as awful. The more likely they are to "make mountains out of molehills".

Here are some questions that can be asked.

B: It's really awful that they did that

D: Why is it so awful that they did that?

Is it awful, or just unpleasant?

Is it awful, or just inconvenient?

Is it awful, or just uncomfortable?

Is it awful like _____?

For the last question, fill in the blank with something most people would consider truly awful. For example, in many

COGNITIVE CHOICES

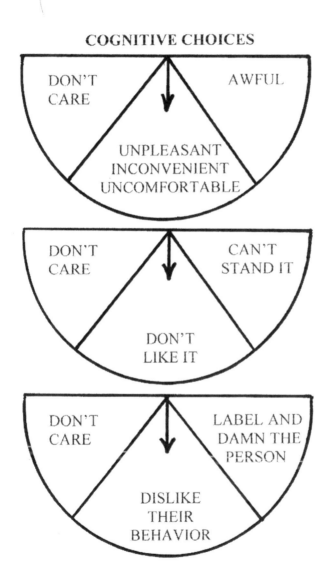

schools, there is unfortunately at least one student with cancer, and that is not doing well fighting it. When students are complaining about some everyday event being awful, there are some simple questions to ask them. Would the student with cancer trade places with other kids who don't have it, and take on all their daily troubles? Gladly. Would those kids trade places with him or her? Would they take his or her cancer to get rid of their everyday problems and complaints? No way. Then why is what's happening to the other kids so awful? The answer is that it's not. It's just unpleasant, inconvenient, or uncomfortable.

People can choose to perceive what happens to them any way they want. However, there will be a much greater emotional consequence for perceiving something as being awful instead of just unpleasant, inconvenient or uncomfortable. Then the question becomes, how is that working for people to look at things that way? Does looking at what happened that way make it easier or harder for them to feel the way they want, or get what they want? Does it do any good for them to generate all the extra emotion? Does it make their life better or worse? Will it be easier or harder to feel the way they want in the future, and get what they want if they keep looking at things that way? People have a choice as to how they want to look at things, and they alone will have to live with the emotional consequences of the way they choose.

The answers to the above questions are:

A: It's not really awful

         It's not awful, just unpleasant

         It's not awful, just inconvenient

         It's not awful, just uncomfortable

         It's not as bad as _____

Something similar to "affirming the preference" can be done when disputing "awfulizing". For example:

ATP: I agree that it's unpleasant when someone does that, BUT...

D: Why is it so awful?

         Is it awful, or just unpleasant?

Another strategy to "de-awfulize" events is to create a physical pain scale, with varying levels of pain from 0 to 100, with 0 being something extremely minor like a pin prick, and 100 being something that would probably be excruciatingly painful, like slowly burning to death. The painful events can be realistic, like burning to death in a car, or farcical like one of Terry London's favorites, "a 1000 paper cuts on your eyeball". (They get better) Then when people start to "awfulize" and magnify the importance and negativity of an event, they are asked to compare it to the physically painful events on the scale. Inevitably, they place the event fairly low on the scale. Then they are encouraged to construct a coping statement like, "Well, it could be a lot worse. At least it's a 1000 paper cuts on my eyeball"

Disputing "I Can't Stand It"-itis

Remember that people have a right to like or dislike whatever they want. The mistake they make is to go from simply not liking something that happens to telling themselves that they cannot stand it. Look at the diagram on page 133 again. There are three basic philosophical positions people can take when something happens. They can take the position that they do not care about it, that they do not like it, or tell themselves they cannot stand it. The implication of thinking and saying you cannot stand something is that you are going to die or go crazy if that thing happened. If people literally died or went crazy every time they said they could not stand something, the streets would be littered with dead bodies and filled with people out of their minds. Here are questions to ask.

B:	I can't stand when they do that
D:	Why can't you stand it when they do that?
	Are you going to die or go crazy if they do that?
	You can't stand it, or just don't like it?
A:	I (you) can stand it when they do that

> I'm (you're) not going to die or go crazy just because they do that
>
> I (you) can stand it, I (you) just don't like it

Something analogous to affirming the preference can be done when disputing "I can't stand it-itis" statements. For example:

ATP: I can understand why you wouldn't like it when someone does that.

I wouldn't like it if someone did that to me. BUT...

D: Why can't you stand it?

You can't stand it, or just don't like it?

"I can't stand it-it is" has become so common and pervasive that we are creating generations of cognitive and emotional wimps. Sadly, it often takes some tragic event to remind people how much grit they really have, or can have if the need arises.

Disputing Label and Damning

The mistake people make when they label and damn someone else or themselves is that they condemn the doer instead of the deed. Refer to the diagram on page 133 again. There are three basic philosophical positions people can take when someone else does something. They can take the position that they do not care about it, they can dislike what someone else said or did, or label and damn the person. People have the right to dislike anything they want to, but when they label and damn the person who did it, they needlessly inflame themselves and the situation, and can make it harder to resolve any conflict and get what they might want.

People have the right to dislike anything they want to, but when they label and damn the person who did it, they needlessly inflame themselves and the situation. Based on this, there are four simple questions that can be asked.

B: He's an idiot for doing that

D: Why is he an idiot just because he did that?

        He's an idiot, or just did an idiotic thing?

        He's an idiot, or just did something you didn't like?

He's an idiot, or just a fallible human being like the rest of us?

A: He's not an idiot for doing that

He's not an idiot, he just did an idiotic thing

He's not an idiot, he just did something I (you) didn't like

He's not an idiot, he's just a fallible human being

Something analogous to "affirming the preference" can also be done when disputing "label and damning" statements. For example:

ATP: I can understand why you wouldn't like what he did.

I agree that it was a stupid thing for him to do...BUT

D: Why is he an idiot for doing that?

Rewriting Demands as Wants, Preferences and Desires

Remember, people have a right to want whatever they want. The mistake they make is to start to think they need something they simply want, to treat a simple preference as a necessity, and to demand what they simply desire. There are two ways to correct this mistake. The first is to dispute, question and challenge the demand. Another is to simply practice writing demands as the Wants, Preferences and Desires (WPDs) they started out to be. For example:

B:	They can't (shouldn't) talk to me like that
WPD:	I don't *like* when people talk to me like that
	I'd *rather* they didn't talk to me like that
	I'd *prefer* they not talk to me like that
	I don't *appreciate* being talked to like that
	I *wish* they wouldn't talk to me like that
	I don't *want* people talking to me like that
B:	They should (have to) treat me better
WPD:	I'd *like* them to treat me better than they do

I'd *rather* they treat me better than they do
I'd *prefer* they treat me better than they do
I'd *appreciate* it if they would treat me better
I *wish* they would treat me better
I *want* them to treat me better

EFFECTIVE COPING STATEMENTS

People have the right to want whatever they want, and like or dislike whatever they want to. However, one of the first lessons in life people hopefully learn is that things are not always going to be the way they want or would like. Sometimes things will happen that they will not like and there is nothing they can do about it. Remember, Dr. Paul Hauck says that whenever people do not like situations they find themselves in, they have three basic healthy options,

1) Problem-solve and assert yourself
2) Tolerate without disturbance
3) Leave

The way to tolerate without disturbance is to think what are called Effective Coping Statements. For example, it can sometimes help for people to remind themselves that they control their own behavior, not others:

No one makes me do anything

It's my choice what I want to do

I don't have to do anything

I always have a choice

I can do whatever I want to

What I do is totally up to me

To be as effective as possible, it helps for coping statements to be short sound bites rather than long convoluted statements. For example, to avoid taking responsibility for others' actions, people can tell themselves:

No one makes them do anything

They don't have to do anything

They always have a choice

It's their choice what they do

They can do whatever they want to

What they do is totally up to them

Instead of making demands of themselves, and feeling anxious, ashamed, guilty or lonely, people can tell themselves:

I don't have to do anything

I can only do so much

I don't have to be perfect

Everyone makes mistakes

Whatever I do is good enough

I'd like to, but I don't need to

I did the best I could at the time

It's nothing to be ashamed of

It won't help to beat up on myself

What I did was understandable

I'm not the first and won't be the last

I'm just a fallible human being

Instead of making demands of others, and becoming angry, people could remind themselves that:

They don't have to do anything

Whatever they do is good enough

They can only do so much

Everyone makes mistakes

They don't have to be perfect

The only person I control is me

They did the best they could at the time

I don't control what others think/feel

I only control what I think/feel/do

They won't be the first or last person to do that

What they did was understandable

They can think/feel/do whatever they want

They're just a fallible human being

Instead of making demands of life, and getting depressed, bored or anxious, people can tell themselves:

It doesn't have to be fair

It doesn't have to be easy

It doesn't always have to be fun and exciting

Life isn't always fair

Life isn't always easy

It doesn't have to be easy

That's why they call it work

No one owes me anything

It won't always be the way I want

I'd like that, but don't need it

I don't have to like what happens

I won't always get what I want

Happiness is wanting what I have (not getting what I want)

Instead of awfulizing, and making themselves feel worse than necessary, people could tell themselves:

It's not awful, it's just unpleasant

It's not awful, it's just inconvenient

It's not awful, it's just uncomfortable

It's not the end of the world

It's just one of those things

It really doesn't matter

It's not that big a deal

It could always be a lot worse

It's over and done with

Instead of saying they cannot stand something, and inflaming themselves needlessly, people could instead tell themselves:

I'll survive no matter what

I can take anything they dish out

I've survived worse than this

I don't like it, but I can live with it

If others can take it, so can I

I won't die just because of that

I won't die without that

It'll be over before I know it

This too shall pass

Learn to bend so you won't break

What doesn't kill me makes me stronger

I can stand just about anything

Effective coping statement can be combined with WPD's.

For example:

B:	They can't say things like that
WPD:	I don't like when people say that.
	I wish they wouldn't say things like that.
	I'd rather they say something nice to me instead.
	BUT…
E:	They can say whatever they want
	The only person I control is me
	It's not really that big a deal
	It could be a lot worse
	I don't like it, but I can live with it
	There not the first and won't be the last

THE ABC STEPS

In math, students are taught that if they approach different math problems in the same step-by-step fashion, they are more likely to get the right answer. So it is with life problems as well. Dr. Ellis created a step-by-step approach to life situations where people otherwise might generate a dysfunctional amount of emotion and behave in a way that makes their life worse instead of better. The goal in following these steps would be for people to get into the best possible cognitive and emotional place to make the healthiest, most rational behavioral choice possible for themselves and others. The steps are:

A   =   Activating Event
B   =   Beliefs
C   =   Consequences
D   =   Disputing
E   =   Effective Coping Statements

An Activating Event can be internal or external, real or imagined. A real event may be a trigger for imagined events. Imagined events are often what people are really reacting to rather than real ones. An REBT therapist might simply ask,

"What happened?"

"What are you imagining will happen next because of that?"

People typically like to ramble on and on about what happened, giving all kinds of sordid details. However, events fall into one of three basic categories. People have been rejected in some way, they have failed in some way, or they've experienced some type of harsh life conditions. Regardless of the details or the type of event, it is the thoughts or beliefs people have about their events that really matter, not the events themselves.

C stands for Consequences, which are what people feel and do as a consequence of what they believe or think about the real or imagined life events. An REBT therapist might simply ask,

"How did you make yourself feel when that happened?"

Notice the question was not, "How did IT make you feel?" because IT does not. Thoughts cause feelings, not events. The next question an REBT therapist might ask is,

"What if anything did you do when you got upset?"

If a person were helping someone else work through these steps, this would be a good place to pose the five questions noted earlier in this book.

What do you really want? (How do you want to feel?)

Did how you felt and what you did get you what you really want?

If you keep feeling, saying and doing what you did, will it be easier or harder to get what you want in the future?

Did what you felt, said or did make your life better or worse?

How did that work for you to feel that way, and say and do that?

It might also be a good time to talk about what, if any, "mistaken" goals the other person might have had.

Somewhere early in the process, it would be important to encourage the other person to have USA, or Unconditional Self-Acceptance, and let him or her know you have UOA, or Unconditional Other Acceptance. It would help to let him or her know that even though what he or she felt might have been more than was necessary or helpful, and what he or she did might have not been acceptable to others and made his or her own life worse instead of better, it was nevertheless understandable. He or she would certainly not be the first person, and certainly will not be the last person in human history to think, feel, say and do something that makes his or her life worse instead of better. He or she has a lot of company, and will have more as time goes by. It is part of being human and nothing to be ashamed of. We are all Fallible Human Beings.

It will often be obvious when people are beating up on themselves for making a mistake, and that the shame they generate is getting in the way of dealing with what happened. This is a sample dialogue of how the conversation might go:

    You: I agree that what you did probably wasn't the best way to handle things, but…

Are you the first human being in history to get upset and do what you did?

Them: No

You: Do you think you're going to be the last human being in history to do so?

Them: No

You: Do you think you have quite a bit of company on this one?

Them: Probably

You: Is it helping any to beat up on yourself the way you are, or just making it harder than it needs to be?

Them: It's not helping. It's just making it harder

You: If a friend of yours did the same thing you did, would you beat up on them, or tell them to cut themselves some slack?

Them: Cut themselves some slack

You: If you can cut your friend some slack, why can't you do it for yourself?

Them: I guess I can

You: Face it, you're just an FHB

Them: What's that

You: A fallible human being like the rest of us who sometimes thinks, feels, says and does things that make his or her life worse instead of better. Welcome to the human race.

The next thing an REBT therapist would do is identify the B, or automatic irrational beliefs that a client had that caused him or her to generate a dysfunctional amount of emotion, and behave in a way that made his or her life worse. The therapist might say something like:

1) What were you thinking when you felt that way and did that?
2) What do you think you were telling yourself?
3) What was going through your head when you got so upset and did that?
4) What would you have to be thinking or telling yourself to make yourself feel that way and make you do that?

It's not uncommon for people to say, "I don't know" because the thoughts they have are so automatic. An REBT therapist might then brainstorm some possibilities and ask the person if any of them sound familiar. For example:

1) Did you ever hear yourself saying something like "They can't get away with that?"?
2) Does this sound familiar to you? "They can't tell me what to do"?
3) Does this sound like what you were telling yourself? "They should leave me alone."?

In an earlier chapter, "scouting the opposition" was discussed. That's what step B involves. It is all about identifying those "enemy" automatic irrational beliefs that cause people to generate more emotion that is necessary or helpful, and to behave in a way that makes their lives worse.

Whether someone is doing this work with and for someone else, or for him or herself, it would help to write the beliefs that are identified down on paper. Typing them out on a computer might be even better, and easier. These automatic irrational beliefs are very fleeting and can be very elusive. They can be like a cognitive cancer, destroying someone without them being aware of it. It is important to identify all of them, just like it is important to get all of a cancerous tumor when performing surgery. When people go to a doctor, they often forget much of what the doctor tells them later. That is another reason why it would be extremely beneficial to write down any beliefs that are identified. Trapping them on paper helps increase someone's level of awareness of their automatic irrational beliefs, and it allows he or she to practice and rehearse disputing them until doing so becomes automatic. Terry London often has clients record their sessions and gives them a homework assignment to listen to the tape one or more times later.

For certain common situations, lists of possible irrational beliefs could be constructed ahead of time and people could be asked to read them and note which sound familiar. For example, as part of discipline procedures, schools could have lists of what are called "hot" thoughts for students to read after they've gotten angry and violated school rules. As noted earlier, having people read such lists and identify thoughts that sound familiar is like running a blood test to find out what is physically wrong with someone. Thoughts that sound familiar are analogous to high or low values on blood tests. It is exactly what is wrong with them. In schools, doing this and working on thinking differently could be offered to students as an alternative to simply putting in their time.

The step that is just as important as step B is step D, or disputing the automatic irrational beliefs. Step D is basically correcting irrational thinking as was discussed in an earlier chapter. Using the computer metaphor noted earlier, it is basically teaching people how to clear the "screens" in their heads of those automatic irrational beliefs that dominate them and cause people to generate a dysfunctional amount of emotion and behave in a way that makes their life worse. It is the defensive game plan that is so often missing in other approaches people are taught to try to prepare them to more effectively deal with troublesome life situations. If someone were disputing another person's demands, it would help to remember to affirm the preference.

Step D is followed by step E, or deciding on some Effective Coping Statements that would help people generate a more functional amount of emotion in the future, and be more inclined to behave in a more rational way. Referring back to the computer metaphor once again, effective coping statements are what it would help for people to have on their "screens" instead of their automatic irrational beliefs. Step E is part two of the defensive game plan.

I've added an F to Dr. Ellis' original steps. F stands for Functional Unhappiness. People may not end up happy about what transpired, but they will hopefully be in a better or more functional emotional place after doing steps B, D and E.

I also added step G, for Generate Options. This is where the simple paradigm developed by Dr. Paul Hauck would come into play. Remember, whenever people don't like situations they find themselves in, they always have three basic healthy options.

1) Problems Solve and Assert Yourself
2) Tolerate without Disturbance
3) Leave (the situation, job, relationship)

However, people have to get into the right cognitive and emotional place to best exercise these healthy options. That's what steps A through E are intended to help them do. Steps A through E are what had always been missing in so many other approaches. Teaching people decision-making skills, problem solving, and communication skills that include how to assert themselves or to refuse others are part of step G in the ABC approach.

If people become proficient at the steps listed above, they will end up at step H, Healthier, Happier, and more Hopeful.

I MESSAGES

"Problem Solving and Asserting Yourself" is one of the healthy options Dr. Hauck has described. The best way for people to assert themselves is with I Messages.

When people are angry, they often use You Messages. You Messages include name-calling, put downs, orders, threats, and demands. They are also called solution messages because they tell someone else what to do and try to impose one person's will on another rather than leaving the choice up to them. People do not like that. They also do not like a finger pointed at them, literally or figuratively, which is what someone using You Messages usually does. These are just some of the reasons You Messages are usually not effective, and often end up being what are called "roadblocks" to effective communication.

I Messages simply give other people information. I Messages tell others what people do or don't like, how they feel (without making others responsible for it), and what they want. I Messages leave the solution up to the other person. People using I Messages are more likely to be pointing their fingers at themselves instead of the other person because they are talking about themselves.

If people can get into the right cognitive and emotional place, they are freer and more likely to access and act on helpful advice and information they have. They are more likely to learn from their own and others experiences, consider potential consequences before acting, and conform to their own morals and values. Most importantly, they are more likely to do what they know is best for them. When people struggle to get into the best possible cognitive and emotional place, teaching them to have an internal locus of control, to recognize and correct irrational thinking, and to approach a troublesome life situation using the ABC steps can be invaluable. These skills can substitute rational thought and effective coping statements for the automatic irrational thinking that caused someone to needlessly generate a dysfunctional amount of emotion, and that fathered unhealthy, self-defeating behavior. After doing the cognitive work, an REBT therapist like Dr. Ellis or Terry London would give clients behavioral assignments to reinforce the attitude change the cognitive work hopefully produced. It is called "Putting your behavior where you want your attitude to be". Practicing expressing dislikes (and likes), feelings, and wants with I Messages would be a perfect follow-up to the cognitive work.

Doing so can sometimes also be a shortcut of the ABC process. It is the same as if people were afraid of riding on an elevator, and they were told to ride the elevator until it forces their attitudes about doing so to change so that they get over their fear. If people simply can utter I Messages, it might have a positive enough of an effect on a situation to get them to change their attitudes toward the situation and people involved and calm their emotions.

There are quite a few common situations teens might be confronted with where they could make serious mistakes. For example, ending up somewhere where their ride home has been drinking and now wants to drive home. After doing the cognitive work to teach them how to get into the best possible cognitive and emotional place to deal with such a situation, I would have students write dialogues to practice putting their behavior where we wanted their attitude to be. I would either give them, or we would brainstorm, a long list of I Messages they could use to tactfully but assertively express their rational preferences and their reasoning for those preferences. I called these life-preserving and life-enhancing I Messages. I even provided very provocative comments for the other person in the dialogue to test them and give them practice at responding to such comments, lest they otherwise be caught off guard or blind-sided by such comments in real life, and capitulate.

The goal was partly to teach them how to best get another person's cooperation. I Message work better than anything else. However, first and foremost the goal was to get them to put their behavior where we would want their attitude to be and hope it would cause them to do what was best for them, regardless of what the other person eventually chose to do. There is an old saying that is taught to spouses and children of alcoholics: "If you can't save the alcoholic, then at least save yourself". That was the ultimate goal of having them put their verbal behavior where we wanted their attitude to be.

For example, if a teen were out with friends who had been drinking and his or her friends wanted to drive home, the teen could say:

I don't want anyone to get hurt or killed tonight

I don't want to die on some country road like others

I don't want anything to happen to you or me

I don't think driving home is a good idea

I don't think our parents are our real problem

I know nothing they could do to us would be as bad as what could happen

I think we made a mistake by drinking

I don't want to make a bigger one by driving home

I don't want my parents to get that phone call all parents dread

I want us all to be alive tomorrow morning

I don't want to go to anyone's funeral, or make anyone go to mine

I'm sure our parents won't be thrilled that we drank,

I'm also sure they'll be glad we called instead of driving

I'm going to do what's best for me no matter what you guys do

I'd really rather we call instead of trying to drive

People can do the same thing with any potentially troublesome situation they might face. People usually know, or at least can anticipate, what others will say in such situations because they have been in similar situations before. This type of verbal sparring with I Messages is called "verbal karate". Anyone who has ever taken karate knows the goal is not to defeat or hurt the other person, but to protect oneself and minimize the damage done to all involved.

Example: Getting a Relationship

Back on Course

Relationships can make for the best and worst of times. People often struggle with relationships. They really want to be close and get along with others, but generate too much emotion, especially anger, and then get into mistaken goals like Power and Control, and Revenge. The behavior that follows often causes the relationship to suffer rather than flourish.

For true long-term improvement and progress in a relationship, people would first learn the skills listed at the beginning of this book. They would learn to have an internal locus of control, unconditional self and other acceptance, and to recognize and correct irrational thinking. Then they would work through the ABC steps for recurring events in the relationship. Finally, they would brainstorm and rehearse I Messages they could use to tactfully but assertively express any grievances they have and try to get what they really want in their relationships. However, even without all the cognitive and emotional work, if they were to simply speak or write the following I Messages to the other person, it also might improve the situation greatly and quickly.

Here are some I Messages that could help people get along better. There is an old saying, "If people do what they have always done, they will keep getting what they have always gotten. If they want different results, they need to do something different." For most people, talking to another person these ways would definitely be something different. Hearing such I Messages from someone else would also be something much different than what most people are probably used to. That would make it less likely that the people involved would slip into their old cognitive, emotional and behavioral "ruts".

There is no set order in which people should speak or write the following I Messages. It will depend on the situation. One piece of information they would want to share is what they don't like.

I don't like when we argue and fight so much

I don't like when we yell at each other

I don't like when we can't seem to get along

I don't like that we're not as close as we used to be

I don't like that we can't seem to talk without arguing

I don't like that we don't spend as much time together as before

Please note that the pronoun WE is used rather than YOU. If someone said "I don't like when YOU yell at me", the other person's automatic response would probably be "Well, you yell at me too", and they'd probably be right. Saying "I don't like when WE yell at each other" will hopefully avoid that exchange. If someone made the mistake of using YOU, and got the retort noted above, he or she could simply agree and say, "You're right, WE both yell at each other and I don't like when either one of us does it to the other".

Note also that the I Messages above are talking about the state of the relationship rather than some specific thing another person has said or done. Hopefully, these would also be dislikes that the other person shares, and something both parties could agree on. Too often, because people generate anger, comments end up being entirely about things that the parties will disagree on. Finding common ground and agreement can be an important step in the right direction, even if it happens to be what both people DISlike. Hopefully, others would respond with "I don't like that either".

When people tell others what they do not like, it helps to also let those others know what they like as well. For example:

I like it better when we get along

I like it better when we talk instead of yell

I liked it better when we spent more time together

I liked it better when we were closer

Part of the information I Messages can share is how people feel, but it's important for them to do it without making others responsible for their feelings. For example, "It makes me mad when you do that" is semantically incorrect and blames the other person for something they technically are not responsible for. The following are some I-messages that might be especially appropriate for young people speaking to parents, but they could work for people of any age, in any circumstance.

I get frustrated when I try to please you and can't seem to

I get frustrated when I try to make you happy and can't seem to

I get frustrated when I try to make you proud of me and can't seem to

I get frustrated when I try to get along with you and can't

I get frustrated when I try to talk to you and you won't listen

I get frustrated when I try to explain things and you won't let me

I get frustrated when I tell you the truth and you refuse to believe me

Even though these I Messages could be very effective, they are semantically flawed. People cannot control what others think, feel, say or do. People cannot make someone else happy or proud, or control whether they are pleased or not. It is the other person's choice alone to make. If someone were trying to please someone else, or make someone else happy or proud, they are trying to do something that's technically impossible. However, these I Messages can still be very effective even if not semantically precise or correct. Some other I messages that give feeling information are:

I get sad when we argue and fight so much

I get sad when we can't seem to get along

I get sad because we're not as close as we used to be

I get sad when we don't talk like we used to

I get sad when we don't spend as much time together as before

People typically respond in a helping way to others sadness. However, it's important to not assume the role of a victim in doing so. Sadness is an understandable emotion for people to have when a relationship they value has not turned out as they expected, or has taken a turn for the worse. However, it is not healthy to slip into a "Poor me" place and to assume a victim role. People always have choices, one of which is to tolerate what happens without disturbance. Another is to leave.

It also helps for people to let the others know they have some understanding about what it is like to be in the other person's shoes. Young people, for example, are often accused of only thinking about themselves and not others. Saying things like the following could go a long way toward dispelling that notion.

I know I do things you don't like

I know I do things that you get upset about

I know I've said some things I shouldn't have

I know we don't always agree on things

I know it's not always easy being my _____ (friend, husband, wife, son, daughter)

I know you mean well with the things you say and do

I know you just want what's best for me

I know there's a lot on your mind sometimes

It never hurts for people to apologize and say they are sorry for any and everything they can. There are a lot of things people could be sorry about or for without apologizing for a specific thing they said or did. For example:

I'm sorry we argue and fight so much

I'm sorry we can't seem to get along

I'm sorry we're not as close as we used to be

I'm sorry we don't talk as much as we used to

I'm sorry if I've done some things you didn't like

I'm sorry if I've said things that you were upset about

I'm sorry if you're upset with things I've said or done

I wish I could take back some things I've said

I wish I could undo some things I've done

It's important for people to finish by asking for what they want. They should temper asking with the knowledge that people don't always get what they want, and they may not this time. But if they do not ask, they will never know. Sometimes it is the way people ask that makes a difference, whether they ask for something in a tactful way or demand it. People do not like giving into others demands.

I just want us to get along

I just want us to stop arguing and fighting

I just want us to stop yelling at each other

I just want us to start treating each other better

I just want us to be closer

I just want us to talk more

I just want us to be happy

I just want us to spend more time together

I just want to hear that you're happy with what I do

I just want to hear that you're proud of me

I just want to hear that you love me no matter what

Hopefully, these are things the other persons also would want. It is hard to imagine they would not, unless they have already mentally and emotionally left relationships.

Please note that the 50 or so I-messages all talked about something that both parties could probably agree on or identify with. Too often conversations between people in conflict end up being all about what they disagree on. Finding common ground would be something different, and better.

One of the best ways to practice I Messages is to write letters to others. When people speak face to face, it is easy for them to plug into their old cognitive, emotional and verbal "ruts" and blurt out something that makes things worse. That is especially true if the other people do the same, and say something provocative. However, when people write letters, they can take things back before others get to hear them. It is especially easy nowadays with computers to correct what people write if it ends up sounding like something that would not be received well and that might only make things worse.

Another advantage to letters is that others will read them,

and perhaps even more than once. This way, people can make their points without interruption, or having to respond to something provocative that might get them off course. And, the more times others read letters, the more likely it is that the points will sink in and have the desired effect. If the I Messages are constructive, and something different than what others are used to receiving, it could very likely make the next face to face meeting much easier and better. For many people, I Messages like the ones above would be so different from what they're used to, that they might even view the letter as a keepsake.

When talking face to face, if things start to get off course and go downhill, it often helps to simply repeat I Messages that have already been said. For example:

You: "I just want us to get along"

Them: "Well then you should think about what you say to me"

You: "I just want us to get along"

Lee Canter produced many helpful programs for teachers and parents many years ago. He coined the term "The Broken Record Technique" for doing this.

Writing letters ahead of time can give people the practice and rehearsal necessary to create "ruts" for using I Messages. That would make it more likely that they could simply repeat I Messages that they have already said, instead of plugging into one of their old, unhelpful "ruts" for You Messages.

SUMMARY

People, no matter what their age, have to be able to get into the right cognitive and emotional place to make the best possible choices for themselves and others. It is something many people of all ages struggle to do. They often generate a dysfunctional amount of emotion because of automatic irrational beliefs they have about others, themselves and life, and then behave in unhealthy, self-defeating ways because of this. Generating a dysfunctional amount of emotion, and what people do because of it, or to deal with it, are important factors in so much that goes wrong in the lives of individuals, families, schools and our society as a whole. That is why emotional management is considered the first and most important life skill.

How healthy, happy, and hopeful, and successful and productive people are now and in the future, depends more than anything else on how they manage what goes on inside their own head in response to their life events. It will depend more than anything else on the theories and hypotheses they generate about how life around them is or should be, and to what degree those theories and hypotheses agree or disagree with reality.

There are five life skills that could and should be taught to everyone, especially our young people, that are currently not being taught. They are:

1) To have an internal Locus of Control
2) To recognize and correct irrational thinking
3) To have unconditional self and other acceptance
4) To have truly effective emotional management
5) A step-by-step process by which to approach any potentially troublesome life event.

In schools, teaching these new skills would not require any new teachers, classes or funds. It would be the quickest, cheapest, and most effective way to really start to target and do something about the real underlying causes of so much that goes wrong in the lives of individuals, in families and schools, and in our society as a whole.

Until such day that these life skills become a regular part of the education that all our young people receive, people of any age can develop these skills by reading, and re-reading the contents of this book. It probably will require multiple readings for some. There is a reason why it is called work. However, if people do the work, it will work for them.